GIRL, PREACH'

A Woman's Call to Kingdom Purpose

TERESA G. LUSK

Nora,
Girl, go preach!
Love,
Teresa G. Lusk

Scripture taken from the New American Standard Bible (NASB) Copyright ©1960, 1962, 1963, 1968, 1971, 1972, 1973, 1975, 1977, 1995 by The Lockman Foundation, La Habra, CA. All rights reserved. Used by Permission. www.lockman.org.

CONTENTS

SECTION 3: ACTIVATING THE KINGDOM PURPOSE IN HER

ACKNOWLEDGMENTS

There have been a few men who have been instrumental in my moving forward in ministry. Some of them hold my full beliefs regarding the girls and their kingdom qualifications while others line up with much of what I have come to hold as my own convictions. Every one of these great men of God has gone out of their way to empower me to preach, teach, and prophesy to the ends of the earth.

I am forever grateful for these guys, starting with Pastor Glen Gabbard. Pastor Glen and his lovely wife, Pastor Diana, were the first few who opened the doors for me to preach during their tenure. Another man who stands up for women's rights in ministry is Pastor Brian M.; I am forever thankful to him for welcoming me in to his church. Along with these great men, I want to thank Pastor Tim Gabbard who partners with me for various events and ministry opportunities following his father's footsteps in making a way for women in the kingdom. Another friend and supporter who deserves to be highlighted is Lloyd Peters, who is one of the first men who inspired me to open up my events beyond women only. Lloyd challenged me to expand my territory, breaking the restrictions of tradition and religion. Bishop Masanje Banda deserves to be acknowledged as the first man who pushed me to become ordained and start our nonprofit. This man became one of my greatest supporters when he saw early on what the Lord had deposited in me. I will never forget his kindness. Thank you, my dear friends, and partners in the kingdom of God.

A special thank-you is due to my friend Pastor Vickie Dubé for reading my book during its early rough draft versions and for the vision she holds for this project. You have been a prayer partner, armor bearer, and faithful friend. Love you!

To my prayer warriors and friends, Pastor Claire Brown, Cara Chamberlain, Nancy Tovar, Melinda Gibson, and Evette Ramos: You bless me! May the Lord repay you for your commitment and kindness toward this ministry and to my family. You girls have been faithful to support the ministry and all its activities in prayer! Love you all.

With love and great gratitude, I want to acknowledge Miss Jackie Mitchell for her faith in the work the Lord has entrusted me with regarding my books. She has been used as an instrument of intercession God's kingdom that has enabled me to dream big and reach high! Love you!

To my sister, Amanda Garza, who is always supportive in word and action in all I do, love you.

Lastly, but equally as important, thank you to my husband, Leon, who has always supported my call. He has bravely stood beside me and pursued truth for himself. Love you!

—Teresa Lusk

SECTION 1

A GIRL'S GUIDE TO BIBLICAL TRUTH

INTRODUCTION

For a few years now, I have been asking the Lord to use me to bring forth a change for the unhindered, unapologetic implementation of women in ministry. After years of experiencing and witnessing for myself the disparity between male and female believers in top ministry offices and positions, I am fully convinced that, unless someone speaks up, this will never change. Taking this topic on is an automatic invitation for unpleasant and violent emotional and verbal reactions and words. However, the freedom that many women and men may receive because of the content in this book brings matters back into perspective regarding the weight of the criticism. This topic deserves another look, much like speaking in tongues; the present work of the Holy Spirit in miracles, signs, and wonders; and deliverance and freedom ministry for the follower of Christ.

I realize that many women have been carrying silent injuries of the heart because of the stance many have taken on women's right to minister in any capacity. While I did not write this book for those who are sold on the idea that women should not preach or teach men, it can still certainly be beneficial to inviting awareness that produces healing.

In this book, you will find examples of great women of faith who preached, taught, prophesied, led nations, had a voice in their marriages, evangelized to entire towns, and more. Let every example address the "why nots" you have been forced to live by and those that you have come into agreement with yourself.

Do you have a pull to minister? Is your most intimate desire to simply be used by the Lord to change lives? To introduce others to Jesus? Guess what? The Lord wants to partner with you and the Holy Spirit here on earth to bring forth His kingdom's purpose.

Do you know who is doing the ministering in nations where Christianity is illegal? It is the women. They are ministering in great numbers to men, women, and children. There is no hierarchy of church leaders, just the true gospel. Women were not the Father's second choice to be used as a voice for Him. For years, we have been convinced that the Lord uses women only in certain situations, especially if a man is *not* available. Do you realize that Satan loves to spread *his* gospel through that false narrative? Imagine a male on his deathbed with no one but a female to share the great news of Jesus Christ with. Would a loving God allow him to end up in hell because another male was not present to minister? Or, what if you are invited to a gathering and a young man whose life is bound by drugs, alcohol, sex, and other addictions needs to hear the preaching of the Word that he may be saved? Will the Lord hold heaven closed for him because there isn't a *man* available to preach and teach him the way of the Lord? We might have bigger problems than our theology if that is what we have come to believe and subscribe to in our Christian faith.

I invite you to look beyond the *familiar* teachings that actually keep others on the highway to hell or hindered from getting a prophetic word or a great teaching because we are divided by two scriptures that have long been abused without looking at the entirety of the Word of God. I personally know great men of God who gave their lives to Christ because a woman was fearless enough to answer to her call when others wanted her in the children's church only. There are also men out there who will tell you that they received a great level of anointing after a woman prayed for them to move in a greater and more powerful flow of the Spirit.

Women, we need to learn to answer to the *undeniable* voice of God. He will not leave you to respond to this great responsibility alone; He will send you a support system even if it is small in number. When I first felt the call of ministry, it was directed toward women first. In time, the Lord brought men into my life to challenge my ministry territory, which caused me to really embrace the fact that I had been called to the nations, including both females and males. When you stop limiting God, the harvest will open up to you. The same Lord who equipped me and called me to preach His good news is the same Lord who works in me to heal, prophesy, and cast out demons. And He wants to do these things through you also. I dare you to stop saying things such as, "That calling is for certain people only." Of course, some of us have been called to a fivefold ministry office, but that could also include you. And, if you are not called to a fivefold ministry, you are still called to minister in some form and capacity. See Mark 16:15–18. Hear His voice when He calls; do not harden your hearts to what the Lord may be welcoming you to do. The Bible speaks of humanity hardening our hearts when the Lord calls us out of darkness and sin as in Hebrews chapter three, but we can also harden our hearts to His call when we fear what people will say. For many of us, the day will come when we will open up our eyes with regret to the opportunities we passed by because someone told us we should not answer as long as we have been created as females.

My heart longs for the time when every woman and man of the Lord will clearly hear and see what I see and hear. The enemy would like to hinder and hold back the kingdom of God. While the Father already has things in place to make sure that the gates of hell will not prevail against His church, you and I will not get to be a part of this amazing kingdom business if we keep turning a blind eye. Ignoring the voice that is calling you and is burning in your heart will not make it go away, so, girl, get ready to preach and allow the purpose of God's kingdom to burn inside you!

On another note, there are some present-day issues surrounding a very demonic agenda under women's "rights." Our rights are to serve the Lord. We, as godly women, can do it without bringing down the men of God. The male-bashing culture that has saturated our nation is not aligned with the current movement of equipping women to progress in the call to serve the Lord. God made male and female; therefore, let us, as women, partner with our brothers in Christ to begin to release many of the daughters who have been so desperately waiting for a supportive, authoritative voice to bring healing, deliverance, and kingdom purpose!

CHAPTER 1

GIRL, IS IT TRADITION OR TRUTH?

I grew up convinced that men were the favored gender of society and even of God. It seemed as if males always got what they desired in status, finances, and relationships. And the only women who could do the same were those who were physically beautiful and manipulative.

This ideology was developed in me through several encounters that started in my childhood. The first experience that shaped my belief was growing up without a father to show me his love, acceptance, security, and favor. The second experience was observing how those people closest to me interacted in relationships with the opposite sex. And lastly, yet most importantly, I learned shortly after my salvation that a large majority of church authority had designated a woman's value—her leadership role in church as well as redemption—to be less than that of our brothers in Christ, simply because she was a female.

While there is a small possibility that this fact is new news to some individuals, there are many women and men who have understood this as a reality that is consistently experienced by numerous daughters of God. We can attribute much of this abuse to incorrect biblical teaching and tradition, the pride of men, a teaching of false humility and submission, a genuine but erroneous belief that the limited leadership role of women is God's will, humanity's need to control, and, finally, the devil's agenda against God's creation.

This subject, like others such as deliverance from demons, speaking in tongues, and the supernatural power of God, have greatly divided believers in Jesus Christ. It is a topic that will require an open heart as we read the Word of God with spiritual eyes rather than the point of view saturated in tradition and past teaching. It will require humility rather than the need to be *right*. It will also require a teachable heart. When we approach this and other challenging topics in this matter, the Holy Spirit of God can work in our lives and through our struggles. The battle for women's leadership roles in the Christian church as a whole is a violent one in the spirit realm as well as in the natural realm. I believe with all of me that the Lord is making restitution for the lack of freedom God's girls have encountered today and in the past. There is an uprising of this promotion as evidenced by the first female clergy to pray at the presidential inauguration in 2016, a woman who also happened to serve as that president's pastor. The Lord could have appointed a man, but He chose a Spirit-filled (charismatic) *female* pastor whose role has been minimized through verbal attacks throughout the web and other media and from many pulpits. In the same way our Father elevated this woman for such a time as this, He is raising up women in other reformative positions in and outside of the church. This is no accident; it is surely not by default due to a man's neglect of his own call as some may suppose.

We must not forget that, despite the fact that women already served in powerful leadership roles in biblical times, I am making the case for a current reawakening. I believe these positions should be filled by women once again and to their greatest capacity. This is something I pray to see accelerated greatly in my lifetime. The Lord has justly appointed her without being inequitable to our brothers in Christ because we were both created by Him and for Him.

In my effort to promote the advancement of women in leadership roles in the church, it is by no means my intention or purpose to reduce men. It is never a necessity to minimize a man, woman, or even a race in order to emphasize the need for redemption of the oppressed. If I took that approach, I would be like those who have been withholding from the daughters what belongs to them. I have two beautiful, strong, godly sons and a loving husband who are worthy to be respected and loved. To reduce the status of a man to less than that of a woman is ungodly, and it would continue to promote Satan's agenda for creation. This spirit of equality is not a competitive, degrading one; rather, it is a rightful attempt to manifest the Lord's heart for women.

I would like to offer a sincere warning that, if this topic and the approach I am offering regarding a woman's equitable right to participate in the kingdom of God and its leadership offices causes a rise of anger on the inside of you or those your share this with, it is time for you to take it to the Lord and ask Him for a revelation of His truth. I say this respectfully as I am not unaware of Satan's schemes, and I understand that his goal is to keep people in bondage to lies whatever they may be (2 Corinthians 2:11). It is time for the church, including the women in them, to fulfill the mandate to bring the kingdom of God here on earth whether she is called to be a minister to the world, an apostle, prophet, evangelist, lead pastor, or teacher, or is summoned to follow any other spiritual responsibility on her life.

Prayer: Father, give me a teachable heart to receive what You are saying in this season regarding women in ministry. Provide for me, by the power of Your Holy Spirit, the scriptures and truths that will set me free to walk into my divine purpose that will empower other women and girls to do the same. In Jesus's name. Amen.

CHAPTER 2

GIRL, YOUR WORTH EXISTED BEFORE THE BEGINNING OF TIME

Women were never a second thought, no matter how scripture has been introduced to you and me by Bible teachers and preachers. While this statement may seem unnecessary, the women who have been deeply violated with this kind of teaching may actually be taking a deep breath right this minute. The *interpretation* of scriptures is often made to infer that God didn't think about creating Eve until he found Adam bored and needing some help around the house. Genesis 1:27 says, "God created man [humankind] in His own image, in the image of God He created him [mankind]; male and female He created them." The Lord created and formed two beings, male and female, and both in *His* image.

Negative experiences in the church or at home, or any other place where a woman learns her value, do not have to have the final say. At the end of the day, every woman has her own responsibility to pursue healing and deliverance if she is wounded due to these injustices.

I like to paint the following picture for anyone who may have doubts about a woman's worth and permission to serve in any capacity within and outside the church walls. When the serpent came around to deceive Eve, he had already crafted his plan. Many regurgitate what they hear in church and state that she was the "weaker" vessel, and they make other incorrect assumptions. I truly believe that, just as she was created differently by the side of Adam, the deceiver knew there was something about and in her that needed to be taken down. As women, we know our nature really well. We understand that, when we are spiritual and love God, we worship mightily, proclaim greatly, stand strongly. The enemy of our souls hates this! Even before we surrendered our lives to the Lord, the warrior spirit was in each of us by His design. I dare to propose that the serpent's cunning visits were probably many before Eve fell to the deception. The reason I believe this is that, while we women are made in the image of God, we are also sisters of Eve. I don't know any women, even naïve ones, who go down by anything in just one try! Do you? No doubt, there was something about Eve that Satan wanted to take down for good, *from the start*. Read Genesis 3:6 again: "When the woman saw that the tree was good for food, and that it was a delight to the eyes, and that the tree was desirable to make *one* wise, she took from its fruit and ate; and she gave also to her husband with her, and he ate."

Adam ate, the Word says. There was no apparent sign of resistance. Satan could have gone to Adam first; instead, he chose Eve. My point is that Eve *must* have had something unique in her that Satan obviously despised in a very special way. And he chose her *for a reason*. It is my well-meaning inference that she had a way of worshiping, or following God, or experiencing Him that was a great threat to Satan.

I have concluded that this has a great deal to do with how women are treated by their own church family at times. And, if I am completely honest for the sake of freedom, some of the worst offenders against women are other *women* themselves. I believe I hear an "Amen!" from many of my sisters at this present moment. I caution my readers and friends against misunderstanding the Word and listening to the enemy's voice. This is how Satan has influenced many people in the church today to misconstrue God's scriptures.

It happens when we have not rightly and fully studied the Bible for ourselves. We have allowed well-intentioned and often the not-so-well-intentioned Bible teachers to settle our hearts on interpretations of the Bible that have plenty of evidence against their conclusions just like at the scene in the garden.

Girl, your worth existed from the beginning of time. We have been on God's mind as His girls, and we have been redeemed just like our brothers in Christ. I like to point out that the same blood that saved my husband and sons and reinstated them as priests and kings on earth, also reestablished me, my daughter, and every other woman as kings and priests. Look at the next two scriptures with me: "There is neither Jew nor Greek, there is neither slave nor free man, there is neither male nor female; for you are all one in Christ Jesus" (Galatians 3:28). And so that we also see that women are also called to the priesthood along with our brothers in Christ, see 1 Peter 2:9: "But you are a chosen race, a royal priesthood, a holy nation, a people for *God's* own possession, so that you may proclaim the excellencies of Him who has called you out of darkness into His marvellous light."

These verses are clear: the Lord is not playing favorites with gender. However, there is adamant teaching against equality even with the clear instruction of the Word of God. Those who deny the validity of equality in this scripture are quick to reply that they agree there is no inequality in God's sight; however, most of the leadership roles are for men alone. Praise God we will have plenty of examples of female spiritual leaders in a later chapter to share with the women and men who are reading this book. This will help to firmly establish God's heart for you, girl.

Prayer: Father in heaven, reveal to me, in an undeniable way, the worth that You have given me from the beginning of time. Uproot the lies I have told myself, those others have said to me, and those the enemy has successfully planted in my heart and mind through my agreement with him. I want to fully recognize that I have never been an afterthought in Your heart, Lord. Release a holy experience through Jesus Christ into the depths of my mind, will, and emotions that will transform my beliefs and my thinking. In Jesus's name. Amen!

CHAPTER 3

GIRL, WHO CONDEMNS YOU?

I remember how I felt shortly after giving my life to Christ; it was as if, all of a sudden, I was pregnant with something alive that was in me waiting to be discipled, trained, equipped, and released. While the seed of the call was germinating, indisputable and uncontainable, it made a few individuals quite *uncomfortable*. Being a baby Christian, I was not necessarily ready to operate in the giftings and offices I had been appointed to, yet the anointing and God's calling would still make its way out of me. This pouring out was much like the way King David, as a young boy, unknowingly trained to be a future warrior, king, and prophet by defeating bears and lions.

Suddenly, right there, in front of the naysayers and unbelievers, a bold word of biblical instruction would gush out of my mouth, leaving the unbelieving in great disbelief. They knew what I was saying was from God, but they had not given me, as a person, their seal of approval. After all, I was a brand-new believer in Christ, *and* I was a *woman*. Women who had been Christians for much longer than I could not believe what the Father was doing in me, and the men who had an oppressive theology would not accept that I was preaching and speaking the Lord's Word. Their wonderment included questions and resistance such as, "Shouldn't your husband be the one preaching? He would be the one to get called first!" Others demanded that my husband must be in ministry simply because I am, or even that my children must also join the call. While all of this *can* be true, it is not always true.

The challenges of being a woman in ministry can be very unpleasant. I have been presented with looks and reactions that were often condemning behind a smile and a word of "biblical instruction," but I knew what I knew. I was different, and the Lord was doing something in me in an accelerated fashion.

Many of God's girls reading this book may be able to identify with me. You may have actually been the recipient of condemning, hurtful remarks in response to Jesus's call in your life, or it may have landed you an appointment with the church leadership regarding the manifestation of your giftings being "too assertive" or "not submissive enough." In response to the condemning behaviors that have been endured by the numerous women made in the very image of the Heavenly Father, I summon you to "Rise up, women of God!" Wipe your tears and exit the pity party, girls. You have work to do!

Though many have cast stones, Jesus is the One at the forefront inviting you to take part in His plan for the unsaved and those in the family of Christ. Godly women and men cannot allow another generation of God's girls to be brought up to deny the call and the stirring in our spirit that has been deposited since the day of our salvation. There are women who have become well acquainted with the gentle yet strong pull of the Lord calling them to take their places no matter the accusatory voices that have been birthed through erroneous church theology and simply a hate or disdain for women. These are the girls I am calling on to *unapologetically* stand and be a voice! Be leaders, be teachers, be trailblazers, girls. No one condemns you!

Prayer: Father, I praise You that I am not condemned but fully accepted in Your Son, the Beloved Jesus Christ. I invite You, Holy Spirit, to heal me from the critical beliefs, words, and effects that condemnation has had on me. I was chosen from the beginning, loved and accepted by the Father, and am now sealed in the Holy Spirit through the grace of Jesus Christ. Your Spirit resides inside me, and from this moment on, I will not hide the person I have been created to be. Forgive me, Lord, for fearing people's opinions and demands over Your will for me. I receive Your healing, restoration, and boldness in the Holy Spirit. In Jesus's name. Amen!

CHAPTER 4

GIRL, IT'S A HUSBAND-AND-WIFE THING

 very popular scripture that has been used for many centuries to oppress women in the church is Genesis 2:18–21:

> Then the Lord God said, "It is not good for the man to be alone; I will make him a helper suitable for him." Out of the ground the Lord God formed every beast of the field and every bird of the sky, and brought *them* to the man to see what he would call them; and whatever the man called a living creature, that was its name. The man gave names to all the cattle, and to the birds of the sky, and to every beast of the field, but for Adam there was not found a helper suitable for him. So the Lord God caused a deep sleep to fall upon the man, and he slept; then He took one of his ribs and closed up the flesh at that place.

The familiar, *unjust*, and *incorrect* interpretation of what we read here has restricted a great number of women and demoted them and their ministries to the simple position of "helpers" to their husbands or to Sunday school teachers for the young ones. If they are "allowed" or "released" to participate in ministry, they must proceed without causing a distraction to their husbands' needs. I meet amazing married women of God who have such a gifting, but it's put in a box in the name of *headship* and *submission* while it is often forgotten or simply unknown that headship actually refers to the *origin* of the woman. This is why we *must* study our Bible for ourselves. This abuse of power has also saturated the church outside of the marriage relationship, from leaders to church members and much more.

My husband has been the recipient of critical talk. Some have said that he is not the "priest" of our home because I am the one who is highly involved in *public* ministry. While my husband has his role in our home as priest, protector, father, friend, and provider, we are *one* in Christ. Both of us have been redeemed and given the commission to serve the Lord on earth as priests and kings. During a deeper search for biblical accuracy regarding the marriage relationship, he took it upon himself to start looking at scriptures closely as the Word instructs. Following is his commentary on the aforementioned verse:

> God created Adam and all the animals from the ground and breathed life into them. When God was looking for a "helper," He brought forth animals. All were made the same, but none were suitable as helpers. This does not mean that God then made *another* suitable "helper." It means that man's mate is not his slave/helper/beast of burden. You can find the word *helper* referring to God in Psalm 33:30 and other scriptures that state that He is our help. So, again, "helper" does not indicate subjection. The woman was created totally different from everything else. She was created from the side. His equal. Not the left side, not the right as the "right hand man." Just equal! Also notice Adam didn't

name her as he did the other animals. He "calls" her woman but didn't name her Eve until *after* the fall in Genesis 3:20.

I asked him at once why he thinks so many people practice this master-and-servant mentality rather than one that reflects a true depiction of husband and wife in the Christian marriages, and he nailed it by explaining that people like to be *in control*. It is easy to dominate a wife in the name of religious teaching, and sadly, this kind of control extends to other religions as well. Think about it for a moment; when Christianity and other religious promote the submission of the wife, there is usually much control in that family. Control was never on Christ's mind. Submission is to *one another* first as stated in Ephesians 5:21. Some parts of the scriptures often are overlooked due to the punctuation, grammar, and division of paragraphs in the English language. If we are all equal, then rules apply to husbands and wives *alike*. Paul gives us a clearer perspective on this in 1 Corinthians 7:4: "The wife does not have authority over her own body but yields it to her husband. In the same way, the husband does not have authority over his own body but yields it to his wife."

This is a very strong statement. A husband is not independent of his wife, and a wife is not independent of him. That is oneness! When people hold a strong conviction of the partisan principles that the wife alone must submit to her husband, but not that he as a husband must be loving and caring for his wife, which includes submission to her as well, the husband can set himself up for pride, rebellion, and disobedience to the Word of God. He may be tempted to dismiss her wisdom, counsel, and blessing in any decisions he makes. If the case for submission is applied only to her, the husband may eventually violate the oneness principle in the marriage framework (Ephesians 5:31–33).

I realize that many may be reading this and finding themselves either relieved or frustrated as I am challenging a tradition that has been used to oppress rather than to bring forth God's will for a wife and even a marriage. Does that mean that I do not regard the instruction for a wife to submit to her husband and regard him with respect (Ephesians 5:22–24)? Absolutely not. I submit daily, and he submits to me because we are one and we have each other's best interests in mind. If either of us were to defile the submission instruction to honor and love one another, which includes submission, then we would only be hurting ourselves and dividing our own house.

Two things can be true at the same time. In fact, in this case, all three scriptures are true: a husband and wife should submit to one another, a wife should submit to and respect her husband, and a husband should love his wife (Ephesians 5). Does the husband not need to respect his wife simply because the Bible says to love her? Of course not. He must love *and* respect her too.

The driving conviction to share this sentiment in detail lies in the reality that, when a man—a husband specifically—is called to the ministry, he is rarely asked if he loves his wife as Christ loved the church. He has an easy go, but when a woman enters into ministry, she is very often put to the test to ensure that she has been submitting and taking care of business at home. I have been in ministry long enough to have been subjected to many different tests. In addition to this, I have observed the investigations other women have withstood in order that they might participate in the kingdom of God.

The church as a whole will have to start asking some very serious questions about this theology that they adhere to so strongly. Is the body of Christ putting the men and husbands to the same level of scrutiny and expectation as the wives and sisters in Christ?

Please understand that this ungodly treatment is not only carried out by leaders who disagree with women in top leadership roles. It is carried out by preachers who actually believe women can be in the fivefold ministry—apostle, prophet, evangelist, pastor, and teacher. Just because they believe in women in ministry does not mean they do not often place the yoke of the "covering and submission" at all costs, and at times, even in abusive situations that I won't get into for now. In fact, I have witnessed men express their expectation of the submission of the wife if she's in ministry, but to this day, I have not heard them speak of their own submission or that of their brothers in Christ to someone else's authority.

If *all* leaders are all going answer to the Lord one day, then why not go ahead and ask them in their initial meetings as they apply for positions in the kingdom of God if they are properly loving their spouses as expected in the same chapter of the Bible that they use to support submission for wives?

If in marriage, the husband is the only one making decisions, and this holds his wife back from ministry, that is not God's will. Even if I agreed that this theological position was correct, it would still be a scary position for a husband to adopt. He should not be able to take the place of the One who decides his wife's spiritual call and purpose.

When those who hold women and wives to a different standard finally get to meet the Lord face to face, will they be able to say that they were free of the sin of *partiality*? Will they confirm to the Lord that they were truly best intentioned when they interpreted the Bible to mean that only men can hold upper-level positions simply because of their gender, even if the crucifixion and resurrection of Christ set the girls free too? Some, in the right environment, will even show gnashing of teeth if anyone rises up to defend women in ministry. This is very telling, and it can point to a stronghold in a person, and yes, even demonic influence.

My plea is to those who hold such strong convictions about one-sided submission, respect, and honor. I remind us all that we are going to answer for every biblical position we take. I encourage many of you wives who know without a doubt that you were called for something greater in the kingdom of God but are limited because of the resistance from your husbands. Keep seeking the Lord for confirmation and positioning! If the Lord has made it clear to you that you are called to a specific office or ministry, then ask the Father to begin to set the tone and circumstances that will eventually move you into where you are supposed to be without you having to knock down the doors or push your way through them.

I have witnessed godly wives stand, pray, fast, be submissive, and live in complete misery because the call and anointing pulls. Some may say, "Well, she is not going to feel that if her husband hasn't approved her call into ministry." That is incorrect! The Lord did not need to consult the husband to decide if He was going to call *His* daughter into ministry. Jealousy, insecurity, fear of the woman abandoning him, and simply, brokenness can often dominate a husband's soul. In some instances, a wife may, in fact, have to war in the Spirit against the very spiritual resistances that rule her husband's heart. It is possible to break it if she does not give up.

Women of God, when the Lord mantled you, He knew you would be married, He knew the challenges that would face you, yet He anointed and appointed you anyway. God is never wrong. Concerning the Lord's proper plan, however, if you have prayed, fasted, received godly counsel, reasoned with your husband, and tried to sit still for unity's sake, then the question that could be like fuel to your determination would be, how sincerely do you want to fulfill His call?

There are times when we are pushed to stand up for what we believe in. The Lord will direct your heart if that is what needs to take place. While unity is the Lord's character, He is also bold and expects His will to be done on earth as it is in heaven. God will teach you to how to stand for something if that is what is required. He knows His son's heart as well, and He will know what you will have to say and do to challenge Satan's plan that is being fulfilled through your husband, who may have a deep wounding from exposure to erroneous tradition and theology.

One thing to keep in mind is that, if you *are* forcing your way through or operating in any sort of manipulation for positioning, I advise you to stop and pray. If it's the Lord, the pieces will fall into place. If it is not, it will cost you double.

Daughter of God, do you need further encouragement? Visit the story of Abigail and Nabal in 1 Samuel 25 in which we see God's hand in a difficult marriage. Abigail, a wife, had to stand up and shift matters because of her husband's foolishness after he upset David. If she had not acted, he would have taken Nabal's life and maybe that of others. Her actions reflected what many in today's Christian circles would consider a lack of *submission* because she took a step without *consulting* her husband; yet, it was the necessary step for them. The Bible calls her a wise woman.

Read Genesis 21 and learn how God told Abraham to listen to his wife, Sarah, when she demanded he get rid of the maid and her son, who was actually Abraham's son too. It was, after all, Sarah's idea that he sleep with the maid and bring forth the not-so-promised child. In His grace, the Lord reinstated Sarah's voice with Abraham, even after she gave twisted advice. If the husband is the only one who has authority and the right to make decisions regarding the wife and the family, then the Lord would not legally (in a spiritual sense) have been able to tell Abraham to listen to his wife when she demanded he get rid of the very drama that she, and eventually he, invited into their home.

And what about the story of Hannah in 1 Samuel 1? God showed up for Hannah, who poured her heart out to the Lord because she did not have a child, which she wanted more than life. The Lord heard her cry. She had a man, but not a child. If the Lord thought the husband was sufficient for her, the child would not have been born. She not only had a child but a child anointed as prophet, a clear picture that, while her husband was important, God cared about the desires of *her* heart as well as his.

My friends, no matter what you hear or what you are taught, remember that the Lord Jesus, the Father, and the Holy Spirit all care about their girls.

There are some women who will pass on their mission for the sake of peace at home, but some things must be wrestled out of the enemy's hands. Obviously, I am not suggesting in any way that we abandon our homes, children, or husbands. The family unit is God's will. I pray you will never be forced to choose between God and a spouse. This, by the way, has happened to some of our brothers in Christ as well. Some of them have been victims of wives who do not want them to fulfill their call and have threatened to leave, or actually have abandoned the marriage. May the Lord strengthen them as well as those who wait on the Lord to move mightily on their behalf.

Prayer: Father, by the power of the Holy Spirit, I ask you to separate from my soul any theological and biblical teachings that I have embraced and adopted that are not in line with Your true desire for me. Your Word states that the Holy Spirit is the Teacher, and I invite Him to teach me what I have been missing up to this moment. Lord, I also pray that my husband's heart will be softened and become obedient toward what You have for me. My heart is Yours, to remain in unity and peace, but also in obedience to You over anything else. Coordinate the public confirmation of my call and position me where I need to be for this office, calling, and purpose to fall into place. Thank you, Father, for releasing Your Holy Spirit and Your angels to minister to me and my situation and to assure me that a breakthrough is coming. In Jesus's name! Amen.

CHAPTER 5

GIRL, THERE IS EVIDENCE FOR WOMEN IN LEADERSHIP POSITIONS

While I was preparing to write this book, the Lord instructed me to draft it a bit differently than most people do when dealing with this subject. His direction was to keep it simple and give you an opportunity to look at a number of scriptures that you may have seen over and again with fresh eyes and perspective. All it takes is to see *one* scripture based on *undefiled* truth to see the actuality in the rest of the Word of God.

In the same way, the Lord wanted to me to provide examples of each of the fivefold ministry offices held by women rather than focusing so much on *defending* the two passages that others use as ammunition.

Anytime people want to resist women in top leadership positions such as that of an apostle, prophet, evangelist, pastor—whether senior or any other level—or a teacher to men and women, they will quote the two most controversial passages found in the Bible: 1 Timothy 2:9–15 and 1 Corinthians 14: 34–35. While anyone can make a case against women leaders by simply reading these *few* Bible verses, a wise person must look at other passages and examples in the Word of God as well.

Here is a personal example of this: My husband and I were

taught over and over for many years that healing of the body was a "special gift" that one must earn. We were taught in a variety of ways that always sounded like truth that healing ministry was only to be exercised by certain individuals. However, Mark 16:15–18 gives us the clear direction that healing as well as setting people free from demonization and going out to preach the Word are all part of the evidence that you and I *are* Christians.

Think back to the garden for further revelation. A simple twist of what God said to Adam and Eve in the garden accomplished the job of deception and destruction for all humankind. In the same way, all we need is a small portion of the Bible to make an entire theology out of what we *want* the Bible to say so that we may maintain a lack of truth and lead others in the same direction. The Word of God is filled with extraordinary women who filled amazing positions but are often hidden by the religious spirits that are and have been in charge of hiding revelations from those who are not willing to find the facticity by studying and showing themselves approved (2 Timothy 2:15). For other members of the body of Christ, these scriptures have not been visible because we have been taught to see only one thing.

Not seeing what *is* in the Word of God is an example of exactly how some individuals who do not understand the *co-heir* truth for men and women and equality in marriage and in the church operate to keep hold of the reins. Then there are those who have been conditioned to never question what they have been taught through their denomination or in the home. Thankfully, today is an opportunity for you and me to do our own homework and ask the Holy Spirit to reveal the error-free interpretation of the Bible and uproot lies and deceptions that have kept women from moving into the Father's will. In turn, this will empower our brothers and sisters in Christ to also see where God has raised up certain women in times past. Let's visit every one of the fivefold ministry positions. Each will provide a clear position of God's heart because, girl, there is evidence of women in top leadership positions within the church!

AN OUTSTANDING FEMALE APOSTLE

There is a female apostle in the Bible, and most of us have missed or dismissed her! There could have been numerous other unnamed apostles and women ministers, just as there were many other disciples who were not mentioned by name even if they were males. This female apostle's name was Junias. Paul the apostle had great women and men of God working with him who actively participated in the ministry. He may have trained them, although they may have already been in ministry. We see evidence of this in the scriptures in the most basic of forms such as a greeting. In Romans 16:7 we read, "Greet Andronicus and Junias, my kinsmen and my fellow prisoners, who are outstanding among the apostles, who also were in Christ before me."

This verse, which describes Junias's position, has not landed on accepting hearts. Arguments have even ensued among resistant and supportive scholars alike. Some have asserted that her name is not appropriated correctly, and they demand that Junias was a male. However, there are biblical academics who have defended her name and confirm that Junias was a woman and that there is not a male version of this name.

This outstanding female apostle's notoriety should not surprise anyone considering all the women that Paul listed as taking part in his ministry in Romans chapter 16. Go back and read this section and ponder on each and every daughter of God mentioned. Read the chapter in several translations, as many have leaned toward the version that favor their heart's discriminations. And, even if you read a scripture that seems to favor Junias as a male, remember to go back and look at all the examples of women in the Bible who were used for God's work. In a topic such as this one, we must do all we can to look at all the evidence that having women in ministry, an unrestrained one that is, is the Father's heart.

Think of this *outstanding* apostle, a female one to say the least. I can only imagine what may have earned her that great endorsement.

Was it her tenacity to stand during persecution of the church? Did she heal the blind and cast out many demons? Maybe she was bold among many who cowered down to the hardnosed religious people much like today. Or did she lead many men and women to Christ? We will one day find out, but we must not underestimate what she must have done to be noted as not only an apostle but an outstanding one. A powerful leader such as the apostle Paul would not have made this kind of distinction to just anyone.

FEMALE PROPHET AND PASTOR

Have you ever heard of Deborah? If you are in the body of Christ, and the Word of God has been read at your church or you have read it on your own, then you must be well acquainted with this woman. She is known as a judge to Israel and a prophetess, honored greatly among the charismatic, Spirit-filled groups. What many have not considered, regardless of their denomination, is that she was also a pastor. In the Bible, a shepherd is synonymous with a pastor. While that title is not often heard in connection with this or any other woman, the Lord is the One who appointed the shepherds in the Word of God. He instructed them to feed His people spiritually and lead them into righteousness as this woman did. Her influence was mighty, and that was not because the Lord could not find a man to fill the shoes as many suggest. No! He chose her and equipped her because He saw her *fit* for the call. In those times, her duty as judge would not be separated from her spiritual responsibilities. That means she directed mostly men for war. She also took care of their souls in matters pertaining to God. Her position has been minimized in many circles because it does not fit their theology and rhetoric about women in ministry. People who deny the equal call of women cannot afford to have any scripture challenged. So how can we prove Deborah pastored? Let's read 1 Chronicles 17:6: "In all places where I have walked with all Israel, have I spoken a word with any of the judges of Israel, whom I commanded to shepherd My people, saying, 'Why have you not built for Me a house of cedar?'"

We must apply the common application of interpretation to this scripture as we would to any other when referring to other shepherds in the Bible. Deborah filled several leadership positions, and she was greatly used by the Lord as a prophet, judge, and *pastor*. Don't forget to go further in your research so that you don't miss other examples of prophetesses who could serve as an encouragement to you and me. Look for Anna (Luke 2:36), Miriam (Exodus 15:20), Huldah (2 Kings 22:14), and other great women of God.

A FEMALE DEACONESS

The apostle Paul said the following about the female deacon in Romans 16:1–2:

> I commend to you our sister Phoebe, who is a servant of the church which is at Cenchrea; that you receive her in the Lord in a manner worthy of the saints, and that you help her in whatever matter she may have need of you; for she herself has also been a helper of many, and of myself as well.

Phoebe was a servant-minister. Contrary to what is often said, she was not serving bread. She was commissioned as a leader to participate in the work of God. She must have been a superb woman of God for the apostle Paul to mention her by name. While serving bread can be a ministry, we must not think egotistically and assign her the bread basket just because she is a female. I personally know countless male ministers who have been servants and helpers to many. Helpers can serve food, yes, but they can preach, teach, counsel, and perform other services. Let's replace Phoebe's name with a male name for a moment. Listen to this: "I commend to you [brother Andrew], who is a servant of the church." Is anyone wondering if he baked cookies and took them to the church? Or do we picture him going straight to the children's church to instruct the little ones while moms and dads received the Word at the main service?

We have been taught to read, see, and interpret anything having to do with female leadership as existing several levels below what any man can do. She is never a minister of the gospel; she is simply a servant of the food ministry, administration, and of course, ministry to children and women. We must retrain ourselves to recognize the Word for what it is even if it makes us uncomfortable when it breaks the rules of our church-imposed traditions. Consider what we miss out on when we reduce what persons filled with the Holy Spirit can do because we reduce them based on gender.

FEMALE EVANGELIST

If the Samaritan woman in John chapter four had been the Samaritan man, would he be well known as an evangelist? Would his faith and zeal be talked about during our Sunday and Wednesday services? I believe the answers to these questions would be yes. Gender has a lot to do with whether or not women will be acknowledged as part of the team of players in the kingdom of God. However, the Samaritan woman is mostly remembered by her supposed "adulterous" lifestyle.

To this day, I have not heard many consider that maybe she was a widow, rejected by her father, or passed on from husband to husband because she was no longer pure according to the expectations of the culture. While it is possible that she had numerous relationships, it is also possible that her relationship status was not by choice. Regardless of what happened, the point is that, simply because she was a female, she is not recognized or identified as an *evangelist*.

If we are honest, many of us can say that we take on a protector role over the Word of God, and we do not allow ourselves to cross the boundaries of controversial scriptures or allow anyone else to, lest we become a heretic. My friends, we ought to be asking the Holy Spirit for His conviction and direction regarding what we have held so dearly for years. I could also use the example of the man with the many demons (Mark 5:11–20). I praise God for freedom, deliverance, and the testimony of anyone whom He has touched, but this man seems to have become an evangelist, and he will forever be known as one simply because of his gender. That's not a bad thing; we just need to be sure we are asserting *godly* equality for all.

In speaking of impartiality, I realize that, with many ungodly agendas in present-day American culture, this could seem like just another form of breaking God's Word and seeing what we want in it so we can live in our sin comfortably and justifiably, calling it freedom and equality. The difference is that we have evidence in the Bible for God empowering His girls for His work.

To parallel a woman serving unrestrictedly in ministry to a lifestyle of sin is incomparable, but it does get treated with the same sentiment by some. Don't allow Satan's busy schedule of pushing forth all sorts of ungodly movements in this season of lawlessness and chaos distract you from what is right and what is not. And, with several forceful and ungodly secular social justice issues being promoted, this could easily get lost in the interpretation of right and wrong. God is calling His girls to position themselves where they belong. His call and your obedience will provide the strength you and I need to say, "Here I am, Lord. Send me!"

FEMALE TEACHER

The last example I will use is that of a female teacher. Her name was Priscilla. Let's dig in to what the Bible actually says about women teaching men in Acts 18:24–26:

Now a Jew named Apollos, an Alexandrian by birth, an eloquent man, came to Ephesus; and he was mighty in the Scriptures. This man had been instructed in the way of the Lord; and being fervent in spirit, he was speaking and teaching accurately the things concerning Jesus, being acquainted only with the baptism of John; and he began to speak out boldly in the synagogue. But when Priscilla and Aquila heard him, they took him aside and explained to him the way of God more accurately.

Can you say, "Wow!" The Word calls this man *mighty* in the scriptures and apparently well taught in the way of God—fervent, meaning he was determined, burning with passion for the Word, and immovable. Not only was he well versed as he held on tight to the Lord, but he apparently taught the Word of God *accurately*, and he was an anointed preacher.

Go back and read the verses line by line and see for yourself! In today's terms, we would say that this man was preaching the house down! So, what could a woman have taught an anointed, on-fire man of God who was filled with the Word? The Bible says that she and her husband took him aside and taught him. My first imperative point for those who say "no" to women *teaching* men is this: if she is not allowed to teach a man—and many use 1 Timothy 2:12 and 1 Corinthians 14:34–35 to uphold this thought—then she should never have taught a male whether her husband was present or not. No teaching and no speaking in church means just that, doesn't it? If we say that she could teach only because her husband was present, then we have already made up our own theology. The woman was gifted, appointed, and anointed, and apparently in a great manner, or she would not have had the ability to teach this man of notoriety. She was not there just for support; she taught, and there is no mincing words about that. Furthermore, she happens to have been named first, and that must be noted even though opposers violently dismiss this as unimportant.

I can grievingly share that many have created loopholes to disqualify women ministers, and I have seen them do it for every single position she could possibly serve in unless it has to do with kids, cleaning, food, or administrative work. Are these scriptures not enough to at least make us take a second look with a humble attitude and understanding that we could be very wrong no matter what our denomination continues to teach today? This type of discrimination has been practiced by Spirit-filled and noncharismatic groups. To add to this disappointment, with my own ears, I have heard *female* ministers state that women pastors are the *exception* because we see only a few real-life examples today. Or they defend their spiritual leadership position by mentioning that their open door to ministry was provided for them only because a man gave up his position for whatever reason. How heartbreaking that we lower ourselves even to the "it was an accident for me to take up this mantle."

Why not look at it in the sense that we see at least one woman in the Word, and that is enough for me! Women are not bewitched or under Satan's curse any longer. We, too, like the boys, were redeemed, and when we read scriptures that seem to limit spiritual opportunities or include restrictions because a person is a female or married, why not ask ourselves if there was something going on during the time of those writings such as the following in (1 Timothy 2:12–14):

> But I do not allow a woman to teach or exercise authority over a man, but to remain quiet. For it was Adam who was first created, *and* then Eve. And *it was* not Adam *who* was deceived, but the woman being deceived, fell into transgression.

Before we point and say "Oh that is clear!" keep in mind that assuming this instruction was for all women, at all times, in all instances would suggest that the woman is *not* redeemed from the curse. We either agree she was redeemed or not. If she was not redeemed, then she should never teach or preach, and she should remain quiet at all times with no exceptions. She will also be in big trouble with Jesus if this is the truth, and so will her husband for breaking God's Word about teaching men. You follow the dilemma? To address the second most controversial scripture regarding women in ministry, the Apostle Paul also stated in 1 Corinthians 14:34–35:

> The women are to keep silent in the churches; for they are not permitted to speak, but are to subject themselves, just as the Law also says. If they desire to learn anything, let them ask their own husbands at home; for it is Improper for a woman to speak in church.

It seems to be all we need to shut the door on women, but as the Lord instructed that I do in this book, I must provide examples of women ministers. Therefore, we must look at a few chapters before this referenced in 1 Corinthians 11:5: "But every woman who has her head uncovered while praying or prophesying disgraces her head, for she is one and the same as the woman whose head is shaved."

Did you catch that women are praying and prophesying? This boils down to a simple matter—common sense. She cannot prophesy publicly if she is not supposed to *speak* in the church. This was a matter of a church issue at that place *during that time*. Go back to all the examples I have provided regarding the work women did. Our Heavenly Father is not confused. He did not allow women to speak, teach, prophesy, evangelize, or anything else in those times and then change His mind toward women today. If anything, the new covenant in Christ—His death and resurrection—truly solidifies the role of women in ministry.

There are many other explanations out there regarding these two restricting passages, but I will not elaborate much on one because the Lord told me to "show the examples" of the women who were unapologetically used by Him. I will add that some scholars say that women were misleading the church and teaching that Eve was created before Adam, and that not having her hair covered suggested she was as a temple prostitute. That is certainly something I encourage you to study. However, regardless of the opinions, we can go back to the facts and examples and leave it there. Stay ready, as this will be a lifelong debate like many other issues.

Now is the time for women to rise up and equip themselves for kingdom business. There is no time to look for approval or to apologize. The summons to revisit the scriptures is not a modern-day, twenty-first-century, get-with-the program demand. It is a genuine invitation to start walking out and adopting the equal godly rights we girls have had all along.

Prayer: Father, give me a revelation of the desires of Your heart for women in ministry, including the fivefold ministry. Forgive me for not being an active participant in Your call. Your desires for me to take part in the kingdom of God can be fulfilled through a specific office, or simply as a Spirit-filled believer in Jesus Christ. Eradicate all false convictions in me, even and especially those that are deeply rooted in tradition and man-made religion. Lord, active me for Your work. I will unapologetically answer. In Jesus's name. Amen!

CHAPTER 6

GIRL, JOIN THE GODLY SOCIAL JUSTICE CAUSE IN THE CHURCH

I am very thankful for the many ways women have advanced in the secular fields in the United States. Women finally have their right to vote and fill governmental offices. They can be movie stars and producers. They can be scientists, or they can start their own businesses and much more. I truly believe that women are being sought after to fill positions that ten years ago or more were not being made as available to them. And just for extra encouragement, we have seen hundreds of strong, qualified women holding positions of influence in President Donald J. Trump's administration. Praise Jesus! How my heart yearns for the day I can say that this is so throughout the globe for all our sisters across the furthest waters.

What about the roles in the church, however? We are greatly lacking support from the men and often the women who have the ability to make changes from within the church walls. We must become the movement of the *godly social justice* cause in the church. While women can and should express their concerns about church injustices that keep them out of certain leadership roles, their plead will never be as effective as those of our brothers in Christ. The men serve as voices of power and reason for us girls. If a woman publicly takes her place and defends her unrestricted call to ministry, she will often be reduced to and labeled as having the spirit of Jezebel. She will be called a rebel or a feminist. In contrast, when a Christian man of integrity, who has studied the Word of God, expresses the truths of God's Word regarding women, many people are more willing to listen. The male has the benefit of not having an agenda attached to him other than seeking to be in line with the Word of God. This does not mean that those who disagree won't make it known to him, but a man's voice regarding this injustice towards women has the power for greater impact than that of a woman—in this present time.

The words *social justice* can manifest a pleasant sentiment or a bitter feeling in anyone hearing the term. This is because many have been waiting for someone to speak up for them for their hurt and pain or because ungodly agendas have been attached to these two words. I ask that, as you read this, you understand that I am speaking only of a godly social justice issue. There are no agendas in my book, simply a desperate call for the men and women of God to heed my urgent reflection of beliefs and traditions.

The current godly social justice issue that needs to be addressed in the church is the indisputable and inequitable treatment of women in the name of God and biblical interpretation.

Brothers in Christ, we adjure you to use your voice for us women who are co-heirs with you and have been given the Christ-paid, Christ-ordained ministry among you. Ask the Lord how you can begin to speak up and *unapologetically* teach those around and under you the truths regarding women in ministry. Would you begin to instruct from your pulpits, books, television programs, social media platforms, and spiritual social circles that God's girls can fill in any capacity, including the position of preachers, lead pastors, teachers, prophets, apostles, evangelists, and ministry leaders in general?

I long for the day when our brothers will stand and let others hear them teach on the Old Testament prophetesses who spoke forth God's Word and prayed or who taught the Word of God to others, including men. There are so many strong examples of women in ministry in the Old and New Testaments; yet, we are not being challenged *enough* by the male ministers who have the influence to do so. I believe that, if our brothers in Christ who genuinely have the theological understanding of women in ministry would begin to voice their concern for the women ministers publicly, they would begin to see the kingdom of God in a greater level of effectiveness. Is this not the heart of Jesus—a true understanding of the kingdom of God and the equality and acceptance of women's ministries?

I have my own conclusions as to why men who know and believe the truth do not step up and speak up. Before I explain them, I will share that, in the same way, women who do not speak up do not do so for several reasons, but the top two reasons are as follows: The first is that they have bought into the age-old spirit of religion's teachings that women have limited access to play in the Father's kingdom. There has been much indoctrination and teaching that has taken root in women so that they feel they will violate God's will should it be any other way. While it makes them sound humble, it is merely the result of a demonic tactic that has run rampant in Christian circles for centuries that has worked to keep women out of the fivefold ministry and beyond. The second reason women do not speak up is the fear of backlash. Women are afraid of getting into arguments and debates with men and other women who viscously attack the ministry of women, often even in their own families. I personally do not enjoy contention; I realize, however, how important it is to share my stance at the right times.

There are conversations that should take place when the grace of God is hovering over a particular moment. In the same way, I believe many Christian men are afraid of the fierce backlash that comes with defending women in ministry. If they do stand for them, they are sure to include the *clause* that women must be subjected to authority and in right standing with her husband. They most often do not leave well enough alone, or even address that fact that a man should also be in proper relationship with his wife before he can participate in ministry. The second reason men stay away from this topic publicly is that they have not had an awakening, conviction, and revelation regarding the pain and injustice women face in the church. A male pastor allowing a woman to preach in his church is simply *not enough* to awaken the body of Christ, although his gesture is greatly appreciated.

Prayer and consistent teaching in this area are necessary to break up the erroneous seeds that have been planted in the hearts of many. There is a great need for sharing loving and consistent awareness from pulpits and beyond. This can release a spirit of healing over so many women who secretly and in plain sight have dealt with cruel discrimination, public ridicule, hidden and public partiality, and more. To be fair, as is my heart, there are a few men who do hurt for women. I know of men who love their co-equals in Christ who have witnessed their wives or even daughters endure the closed doors and hate because they are girls who know they are called to minister *unrestrictedly.*

As it is with any social justice cause, if we believe in the need to correct something because it hurts the Lord's heart, our voices must be heard. Engagement and awareness are every believer's responsibility. This situation is a burden for me to bring to light as I summon those who have ears to hear to join me in this call for awakening. My plea is for and about all the women in the church who have been kept from fulfilling their God-given purpose and call, for those who have fulfilled it with great disparity, and for those women who will come after me, including the women who will read this book—our daughters, granddaughters, and our spiritual daughters.

It won't be an easy task for those who are willing to take on the cause, but grace will be made available to those who will rise up. There is often much warfare enveloped in this cause, just as there is with other controversial topics such as speaking in tongues and the present supernatural power of God. The demonic struggle and resistance surrounding this subject is a glaring revelation of the forces of darkness that are behind women who dare to answer their call as ministers.

My brothers and sisters in Christ, will you please take this cause and run with it? While I could call on the brothers alone, and women do need their public support, it takes women to sink into the identity in Christ, and an unapologetic call of God to start making a change as well. If the men start speaking up, what good will it do if the girls stay back!

Prayer: Lord, I want to be used by You to defend those who have not been seen or heard. Use me, Lord, to bring forth truths wrapped in convicting love for the sake of Your kingdom. Give me an overflow of boldness to speak when necessary and to remain silent when You instruct. Father, fill my mouth with words of grace as I challenge oppressing and false theologies that have held back Your daughters, including myself. Cause me to rise up and walk in the fullness of who I am in Christ. And when the accusations come, I will watch You rise and stand before me. Lord, let me not speak out of arrogance or a need to be right, but simply because I want to reveal a truth. So it shall be! In Your name. Amen!

CHAPTER 7

GIRLS, THERE'S ROOM FOR YOU TOO

While I was attending graduate school, I made a friend named Mary. This sweet young woman had a father who loved her so much, and he showed such care in so many ways. As an outsider who did not grow up with a father, I was really touched when I witnessed Mary's relationship with her dad; it warmed my heart. At one point, I expressed to her how blessed she was to have him, and her response was so sweet. She *offered* her dad to me if I needed a father to advise me. She said I could "borrow" him! I believe that the most touching aspect of this was that she was serious.

It has been a blessing to me as well to observe my husband, Leon, be such a good daddy to my daughter and sons. He is loving, kind, gentle, and can also discipline well. Men, fathers, and male leaders are much needed. The Father in heaven never intended for us to not have our earthly dads present with us. Unfortunately, sin and brokenness, and simply unfortunate circumstances have left many children to grow up without a father.

As I have grown in my walk with the Lord and in ministry, the Lord has put several God-loving men into my life who have had my best interest at heart and who have given me advice, direction, prayer, and support. They have, in many ways, been spiritual fathers, and they have fathered me through different times. Their force has contributed to my expansion as a woman in ministry.

All believers benefit from having a spiritual father at their side to help train them up and direct them in some manner. Although I believe in the importance of an earthly father, I must say that a mother is equally important.

I have observed a preference in language and suggestion that, when people need to grow spiritually, they need a spiritual *father*, but a mother is not as often emphasized. The acknowledgement, or lack thereof, has been made by both those who believe in women in ministry and those who do not. This points to the possibility that there are some honorable men who may not have considered or are aware of what they are saying, or in this case, not saying. They may not be stating the fatherhood-*only* idea to be exclusive, but we need to include a more kingdom-inclusive partnership in language. This awakening matters because this is language that can heal or hurt.

I do believe some ministers have been saturated in a male-dominated evangelical world. Awakening to their unintentional, unequal leaning will require that someone speaks up to bring their attention to this situation.

Every one of us has been in need of a natural father and mother. If one parent is missing, then we do not always benefit from all that life has to offer according to the Lord's will. A mother cannot give to a child what a father must, and in the same way, a father cannot give a child what a mother should here on earth. That principle is the same with spiritual fatherhood or motherhood.

Ministers of the gospel, I adjure you to remember that the Lord uses spiritual mothers as He uses spiritual fathers. When we are equipping members of a group or congregation, let's remind them that they need *both* in their lives. In our ministering, can we remember that the mothers were also qualified by God to birth forth women and men of God to their posts and purposes? Mary, Jesus's mother, is, after all, the one who ushered Him into His first miracle (John 2). There is power in both spiritual and natural mothers. In our preaching, can we not only tell the congregants that they need men of God in their lives but also women of God? Better yet, can we just exalt the Lord and tell them they need Him more than they need us? I use this example because it is very common. It's real, and men and women can relate to it if they think back on how prevailing this is in the church.

Becoming aware of the way we communicate an idea can really provide an opportunity to begin the healing process for those who have been left behind or left unacknowledged. The words we use must go beyond the *spiritual father and mother* example.

Another form of language that continues to enforce the inequality in female and male ministers is when we describe the great "men of God" whom the Lord Jesus has used to do great miracles, signs, and wonders. Yes, there are, have been, and will continue to be wonderful men who have been used in a mighty way, praise God! Also, there have been great women of God. We must remind the church as a whole, as we reminisce about what God has done in the distant and recent past, that the Father has qualified, equipped, and released many women, and because of that, we *all* have hope that we might be used on the earth! Can't think of any girl preachers off the top of your head? How about Evangelist and Pastor Aimee Semple McPherson, Apostle Heidi Baker, Evangelist Mariah Woodworth-Etter, Prophet Cindy Jacobs, Teacher Marilyn Hickey, Pastor Paula White, and so many more who are not often noted as *spiritual mothers.*

Once we become aware, we can change tradition, empower the church, and equip the saints (Ephesians 4:12). Let's make room for the girls! They will be forever grateful!

OPPORTUNITIES THAT HEAL

Language has left out so many sisters in Christ who honorably serve God and His people right next to our brothers. We must become aware of the number of women ministers who have not been invited to take part in what the male ministers are doing. Go back in your memory for a bit and try to recall the last Christian event you may have attended that was for the general public, not specifically for women or men. Was that event dominated by males? Were the number of women serving in the minority or in minor roles? In the same way, are we as women keeping this in mind regarding our men preachers? We cannot deny men the right to minister alongside us just because a separate group of males denied us the rights of the kingdom.

I truly believe that you must open up doors for yourself when you cannot find one open to you—as long as the Lord gives you the blessing, so please do not misunderstand me. I am not demanding that everyone must begin to do something out of obligation and fear of being accused of being misogynists. What I do stand by is calling the church of Jesus Christ, which is mostly led by men, to start leveling out the playing field of the kingdom of God in the way they speak, make room for, and publicly support their female counterparts. If our brothers begin to consider women of God *qualified* to preach, speak, teach, be on their program, and fill positions of equivalent responsibility, this will begin to take root for many others who are waiting for someone to give them permission to include the sisters in Christ.

My plea to those who can hear the heart of Christ behind my call will answer. We girls thank you in advance!

INFLUENCED BY GENDER

Consider this moment my invitation for all believers. Both men and women are invited to host a self-survey on how they interpret the level of importance of the female figures referenced in scriptures and the room we have or have not been willing to make for them.

The first example we will point to is Mary, the mother of

Jesus. This woman is often remembered at Christmastime for her willingness to ponder what the Lord said to her regarding the conception of the Lord Jesus Christ (Luke 2:19). On Mother's Day, Mary is also given credit for her suffering as a mother. Beyond those two common acknowledgements, have you personally noticed this woman being celebrated as we do men of God such as King David, Moses, Elijah, Daniel, and other biblical male figures? Most of us limit our recognition of Mary's life and influence to two holidays, each of which comes only one once a year. We must hear more often about the admirable and relatable characteristics this woman had. She had to possess a mighty faith like Abraham's to see her promised Child birthed. She had to have humility like Moses's when she was talked about for her mysterious pregnancy. She had to find great strength, like no other woman in the Bible, to be able to witness her Son being beaten, bruised, and crucified. Mary was used for an unlikely miracle! Men and women can find strength in her success to overcome great challenges.

Let's begin to cross the lines of gender, tradition, and generations so that we may benefit from the fullness of her story, and let us find many other female biblical figures in the same way such as Naomi, whose story is told in the book of Ruth. Naomi was one powerful mentor, but she is mostly credited with teaching a young woman how to get a man. While she deserves acknowledgement for her work in that area, let's not miss the gems of understanding this woman possessed. Naomi, like Mary had an iron-will determination. She was quick to plan her life in the midst of great loss and devastation. Before the death of her two sons and husband, Naomi was known as one who was pleasant to be around. She was a woman of strong standing, and her family was well known. She possessed an understanding of culture and strategies for dealing with the past, the present, and the future. Naomi was willing to foresee beyond the loss she endured, and her wisdom about the rules for life in relationships is glaring. Any person would benefit from a thorough look at and application of the principles she mastered. Relationships are not the only thing she was brilliant in; she knew how to position a person to snatch back what the devil stole and many times over that! Don't be afraid to break the rules that limit and withhold the gems awaiting you from this woman's life. Once we get a glimpse of what we have been missing, our eyes will be open to so much more that we may even grieve over what we may have been missing out on for so many generations.

Prayer: Lord, forgive me for not being willing to open my spiritual eyes and study Your Word in greater depth, that I may find the evidence of Your purpose for women and for their right to participate in the kingdom of God. Your kingdom is for all Your children, and I ask You to teach me how to take my own place and show others how to answer to theirs. Father, in Jesus's name, please give me an awareness in the things I say and do, that my words and actions begin to bring healing and awareness to the issues regarding women in ministry. Let my words heal me and my sisters in Christ. Give me the heart to provide equitable opportunities for them to join me and the men who have been partaking in the kingdom of God, that Your will may be done here on earth. In Jesus's name. Amen.

CHAPTER 8

GIRL! STOP PROMOTING THE DEMONIC AGENDA

have mentioned several times throughout this book that women can often be the greatest transgressors when it comes to disqualifying their sisters in ministry. How is it so easy for one woman to resist the elevation another? We learned early on that women who do not support the daughters of Christ in ministry may have been raised in an environment since childhood or through her church to believe that women are to be limited and we are to enforce it. Maybe she wasn't raised this way but took to a particular pastor who had great messages but had a strong theology against women and then she made it her own. The reasons area varied and more than enough.

As women, we have a responsibility to awaken to what Satan has been successfully doing since the beginning of time in the garden. Remember, he came to Eve first and brought her down and everyone else with her. To this day, there is a fallen-state mentality toward women that they are still deceived; therefore, her spiritual influence should be minimized. This is Satan's agenda. He will use anyone as long as he can keep her from participating in the kingdom of God. Have you ever wondered why? I caution my sisters in Christ that, if this is your position, you should evaluate carefully through prayer, greater study in the Word, and exploring more than just your own church's advice or that of your Christian circles.

There is something Satan would like to take from women, and that is her entire call and purpose. I remind you that Satan could have dealt with Adam, but he was no fool; he went for Eve.

Awaken, oh daughters! Ask the Holy Spirit to reveal to you what else the enemy has been trying to steal from you from the beginning. And, in the authority of Christ, command that all that has been stolen must be given back to you. Was it your child's salvation? You can demand it back. Is it your health? You have a right to see your body healed! Is it your own call in ministry because of your own theology? Take it back! Don't wait on your man to do it for you. Women have been led to believe that their authority is less than that of their husbands, and therefore, they cannot pray and demand that what is theirs must be returned by the deceiver. This too has been done in the name of religion while we have blindly continued to promote Satan's agenda. The enemy would love it if you prayed less and waited for your husband, or any man, to "get right" with the Lord so that what Christ has already paid for at the cross and resurrection can be released to you. What has been given to us has nothing to do with a person.

Sisters in Christ, both single and married women must take hold of the truth! What the Lord has gifted us with was not conditional or attached to a spouse or a church official. This is true of men and of women. If you believe that you are waiting on a spouse to get right before the Lord can use you, so it will be as it will be done according to your faith (Mathew 9:29). There are blessings that will manifest when there is unity in a home, a marriage, an organization, or a church. I am not denying that this concept, however, *can* be applicable if you are married. Some ministries are couple oriented, no doubt. However, the Lord has work to do, and He will work with a willing and ready vessel. The Lord will work within a marriage and also through single men and women. Please take a moment to reflect on the weight we put on women compared to that we put on men.

Men in ministry, because of religious people, never have the same requirements to meet. So women, begin to be like our wonderful brothers in Christ and sink into the truth when you are called to answer to the Lord. Equip yourself with truth *for you* so that you do not waste time engaging in agreement with the accuser and defiler of your future regarding this topic.

Part of the devil's hate toward you and me has to do with the fact that we are made in the image of God. And I want to paint a more detailed picture for you so you can understand what this really means. As Christians, we have been trained to constantly picture the Father as a male figure; there is no room for a feminine image. To even consider that the Lord may possess both male and female qualities may make some cringe, but my point is that, for a woman to exist, she has to possess something that is part of the feminine image of God if He created male *and* female in *His* likeness. Think about it! The woman possesses the fullness of God in her, and the enemy knows that even more intimately than she does at times. The image of God is not just what He may look like to *us* as humans. We can agree that the Father is protective, strong, and a warrior. He is worthy of honor, worship, and respect. And these are a few of the male characteristics of God and of many if not most men. God is also tender, compassionate, and willing to express Himself and His love, much like His girls. All these characteristics are part of God's essence. There has to be a male and female portion in God so that both girls and boys may be able demonstrate any of them. The revelation a woman grabs a hold of or lacks regarding the male and female being of the Lord will determine whether she stays in place or advances in her call. A blinding to this understanding, especially in the church for centuries, claims responsibility for this unfortunate reality and her lack of participation within and outside the church walls. If a woman is not participating here on earth through the Holy Spirit, in her God-given anointing, then the gospel is not complete and we cancel out Joel 2:28: "It will come about after this That I will pour out My Spirit on all mankind; And your sons and daughters will prophesy, Your old men will dream dreams, Your young men will see visions."

There is something in her that only she can release; it is the same with our brothers in Christ. Just as the full gospel must contain the supernatural power of God through the Holy Spirit and include preaching the Word, and miracles, signs, and wonders to be fulfilled, so must males and females serve the Lord without constraint. Yes, the Lord will still get a portion of His work done just as many are saved and then pass away without ever seeing a miracle in their lives. This does not mean the Father intended it to be this way. He commanded us to experience His fullness!

In my ministering, I often talk about religious and pharisaical spirits that try to resist the present-day miracle-working power of the Holy Spirit. In the same way, I dare say, are the same spirits that hold women back today. Girls, break up with Satan's agenda and stop promoting it. Repent for the active participation in holding your sisters back. After long centuries, we should have learned something very powerful from the men, and that is that they hold within a natural ability to be loyal to the brothers, even at a young age. Let's practice the same in the name of promoting God's women for the work here on earth! Now repeat after me, "Satan, I break up with your agenda for me and God's girls!"

Prayer: Father, I repent for not supporting my sisters in Christ and agreeing with Satan's agenda to hold them back in the mentality of the fallen state from the Garden of Eden. You chose us as women to serve and love You and to teach others to do the same. I renounce not getting a hold of my own call and considering what You have asked me to do over the desires, opinions, and traditions of others. Set me free, Lord! In Jesus's holy and powerful name, I pray. Amen!

SECTION 2

THINGS GIRLS NEED TO KNOW TO GO DEEPER

CHAPTER 9

GIRL, ANSWER TO YOUR UNLIKELY CALL

My husband and I gave our lives to Christ in September 2003. A pressing issue led me to contact a church near me, and they invited us to join them after a time of prayer and encouragement over the phone. There we were, a blended family in a new town, trying to make a better life. We were received by a loving pastor who wanted to lead our family to the Lord. When that pastor gave the altar call, we knew we had to answer.

Instantly into our salvation, we knew something was different, and eventually our little family received the baptism of the Holy Spirit with the evidence of speaking in tongues. While we were not living our lives in the same out-of-control manner we had experienced before we were married, there was a great residue of brokenness that begged for healing and deliverance. We passionately hungered to read the Bible, we were at church every time the doors were open, and we had a joy that we had never experienced, even through tough times.

A few months after this new chapter in our lives took off, I began to feel a stirring in my spirit that I could not explain. I would watch powerful preachers of the Word such as Pastors Paula White, Jentzen Franklin, and Creflo Dollar along with Bible teacher Joyce Meyer and more. These preachers fed me the Word of God and were not afraid to teach in a way that would offer encouragement and conviction all at the same time. Self-help preaching had no room in that season of televangelism! I read book after book on Christian growth and topics of that nature, and I began to pursue all things Jesus with an unrelenting passion.

Within a few months, the Lord spoke to my spirit and told me I would be working with women in ministry. While I didn't get all the details of His plan, I had enough information, so I began to share it publicly and let people know the Lord was going to use me. This was a premature move on my part, no doubt much like Joseph in Genesis 37 when he shared that, in a dream, he had seen his family bowing down to him and needing him for survival. Years later, I am certain the insight the Lord gave me was to prepare me, but in my immaturity, I misused it. Thankfully, the Lord is graceful, and eventually I learned discretion.

The call on my life was only the beginning, however, as the Lord and I began a major reconstruction process within me. There were years of learning the Word, emotional healing for past and present wounds, humility and character development, training in faithfulness, and so much more. Every period of growth for public ministry required a season behind closed doors of separation and preparation.

The life I had led before coming to Christ left many with disbelief that I could have been transformed to such a degree. Family members and friends were acquainted with a woman who had many issues and could use some serious help. Even in my need for growth and maturity, the Lord Jesus still used me in the areas of speaking and training. For years, I would also visit women's groups and share my testimony titled, "From Darkness to Light." Or, I would visit moms' groups and train on any topic that encouraged women in the home. This season lasted a good while, and I learned so much about myself, others, ministry, and what the Lord expected of me.

Once I got certain life and ministry principles and habits down, my ministry began to expand to not only women but men too. After

I had spent some years ministering and speaking to women only, the Lord expanded my territory, and men would ask if they too could participate in the meetings I was holding or events I was speaking at. All of a sudden, I considered that the ministry that had been entrusted to me was no longer for *women* only. This call had evolved, and there were men and women who needed to hear the messages the Lord was giving me as he had anointed me to preach.

As I took a step of faith and considered that my messages and ministry were for all, the Lord began to open doors with all types of audiences. God's girls and boys were being touched, healed, delivered, and encouraged. Praise God! I thank the Lord for the male voices that encouraged me by asking if they too could partake in our ministry events. They believed that what I was entrusted with was for *all* God's children. I will never be able to repay those guys for such a gift.

I don't know where the Lord started with you and where He will finish, but I do understand that His plan is constantly being manifested at the proper timing for the good of all. When you lean your heart on Him constantly, your only result is to watch His will played out in your life. Of course, not everyone will celebrate the evidence of His calling on you, but the call is from Him and for Him.

So, girl, what does your unlikely call look like? If you trace the steps of your journey, you will find Him directing you even through the resistance or in quiet seasons. This unlikely call of mine has opened the door to critics and unbelieving believers, but it has also set many free, baptized people in the Holy Spirit, healed the sick, cast out demons, shared the heavy glory of the Lord, and poured out the love of God. This unlikely girl with an unlikely call will continue to preach! Will you?

Declaration: I decree that I have an unlikely call in Jesus. Neither my past nor my present can stop it! Critics cannot hinder the call! The plan of the enemy cannot hold me back! I serve a mighty God who has and will continue to be served by unlikely people who have hearts after God's own heart.

CHAPTER 10

GIRL, YOU ARE ANOINTED

irl! You know you are anointed or you would not be reading this book. Your anointing compels you to seek more and find out how you can serve such a loving God who dared to pick you to represent Him and His kingdom here on earth. This anointing is your call to kingdom purpose. Amen! Beyond the call, it is your approval and permission to jump in like never before. Position yourself, woman of God, and start operating by the faith you *already* have; the anointing will take care of the rest. Anointing has a purpose and a subject. The faith you possess provides the unseen substance of why you fervidly pursue the two, even when it doesn't make sense to those around you, or sometimes even to you.

If your history includes a relentless chasing after something that won't leave your mind, you're anointed. If you can be found faithfully seeking to remain in the pursuit of all that this call entails, that is the anointing driving you! I can't help but to preach the Word. Whether in person, on video or television, or in a book, it cannot be shut down. And if I do have to shut it down for any particular reason, I begin to grieve and experience depression of some sort. The gifting in you, powered by the anointing, cannot be silenced without a consequence.

Even those who have gone astray and are running away from

their assignments will occasionally and regrettably ponder on what they know they are supposed to be doing. The anointing for a call, a mantle, or a position, will make itself known, and neither you, your foes, or friends, will be able turn a blind eye to it. Anointing shouts, it pulls others in, it manifests in the natural what is revealed in the Spirit. The anointing is the spiritual rubbing that exudes the essence and presence of Jesus in any particular way for the will and purposes of the Father through the Holy Spirit. And when that anointing is allowed to be released, people will desire or deny Him (2 Corinthians 2:15). Regardless of the decision an individual makes when subjected to the anointing, it does what it is supposed to do—it draws people in and causes them to see the Lord!

This spiritual smearing and stamp of approval called anointing will manifest itself in you, and you will witness people's excitement over your holy assignment as you deliver hope and an awakening to their destination, or an answer to a longing they have been carrying. This commission may welcome a response that looks like a curiosity that lingers in people when they hear you preach, teach, prophecy, edify, correct, rebuke, exhort, govern with your words, intercede, or do other spiritual works.

The proof of your anointing may also be linked to the way you raise your kids, build furniture, play a musical instrument, lead worship, build a team, and so much more. Anointing will impel others to want to know more of what makes your ability so mesmerizing. Your willingness to carry on in the anointing will provide an opportunity for men, women, and children to meet the Lord if they are not believers, and to see His glory made known here on earth for the saved and unsaved. What an honor to live this out and carry the very Holy Spirit that reveals Jesus here on earth and draws many to Him while using our God-given gifts. Is that not amazing?

He gifted you and anointed you. He decided to use you to impart Himself to others. This blessing has been given to men, women, and young people who receive Jesus Christ as their Savior and Lord, and no one is cut short.

Girl, you were given the same measure of the Holy Spirit that any of our brothers in Christ have received. The anointing given to you has nothing missing, nothing lacking, and nothing broken. It is within you in its *fullness*. If we understood the completeness of this privilege, we would never seek to limit or hide it just because we are women. Once you operate in the anointing in the presence of the body of Christ, whether while preaching, teaching, prophesying, casting out demons, praying, pastoring, or evangelizing, you will experience such a heavenly authorization that the Lord is not looking at males and females to quality their call. He is looking simply for those who are anointed to serve (Galatians 3:28)!

Declaration: Anointing was the Father's idea, and He anointed me from the beginning of time. The powerful flow of the Lord Jesus Christ exudes from my being. He heals, restores, and draws many to Himself when He reveals Himself through the anointing placed within me by the presence and power of the Holy Spirit!

CHAPTER 11

GIRL, GET YOU SOME DELIVERANCE

As soon I accepted the Lord as Savior of my life, I was immediately accepted in the Beloved; I wasn't working to earn it (Ephesians 1:6–7). I was sealed for the day of redemption (Ephesians 4:30). I was forgiven. I had access to all that the Lord had given me, for which He had paid through the cross and resurrection, and from early on in my walk with the Lord, He took me through *seasons* of healing and deliverance. I didn't ask for it when it first started. He ushered me into it to prepare me for Him and for ministry.

Once I experienced the power of His healing and freedom, I began to welcome it, and I wanted nothing less even if it hurt to heal. The best experience you and I can live out is the God-ordained, self-willed season of inviting the Lord to deal with the carnal and the demonic that hinders our lives. This is such a big part of preparing for ministry, and many can testify to the power of the freedom that comes with this experience.

Don't allow anyone to steer you away from the deliverance of the Lord. While the keys to your freedom have already been given to you, just as you did with salvation, you grasp for your deliverance. Some healing and freedom manifests at the moment of salvation, and some presents itself later when we become aware that the freedom is our gift paid for by the Lord.

Those who often seem to need the most healing are individuals who subjected themselves to witchcraft and false religions or have indulged in heavy sexual activity outside of marriage, as well as those who may have suffered abuse of any kind. This does not mean that, if you didn't participate in or experience any of this, you will not need it; those are just the people who most certainly will be in need of freedom ministry. For others, the evidence of the need for healing and deliverance may show itself as deep jealousy and insecurity that will cause them to sabotage themselves and those around them. These individuals are known to participate in a secret competition that only they, the Lord, and the discerning can see. Their brokenness may also look like the gossip and murdering of character that so many subscribe to because their insecurities have overtaken them. Sometimes deliverance is just a cleaning up of your character by the Word and power of God, and at other times, it is a dramatic face-to-face encounter with the enemy of your soul who has been there long enough and will not voluntarily leave.

This is why not fully facing and dealing with our brokenness *can* restrict the flow of the gifts, and there can even be an inner struggle of some sort that seems to always be present. The neglect of facing our issues may eventually manifest as repetitive nightmares, feeling as if a presence is making itself known while we are sleeping, or a consistent encountering of closed doors. This does not always apply to every single individual, but I have witnessed that these are sure signs for requiring deliverance. The Holy Spirit will reveal the need for healing in you and me; all we have to do is ask Him. And sometimes we don't ask Him with our words, but eventually the pain of the bondage and hurt becomes enough that our spirits will cry out.

I caution you not to hide from your own need to face some things. Human nature will assume the best in ourselves, so it makes it easier to find the brokenness in others. When I first became a believer, I thought all those around me had drama in their lives except for me. That false humility and the "I'm in the Lord so I am good" attitude put me at a disadvantage. When the Lord opened my eyes, I was a little embarrassed and greatly disappointed. I had wasted time looking at the specks in others' eyes while the log in my own smacked others in the face.

We will all continue to grow and heal as we go, so most of us will minister to the world and the people of God even in our own need for more restoration. However, if you humble yourself and ask the Lord to begin the healing work that only He can do, you will see ministry flow in a more powerful way than you ever expected. As Christians, especially in ministry, we must guard our hearts from allowing pride, eloquence, and our years in the Lord from becoming real, reflective, and transparent with ourselves. There will always be discerning women and men of God who can see right through us. And the Lord in His mercy will allow us a time to decide to reach out for His healing and freedom, but if we don't, it will eventually make itself known *publicly*. I have met powerful ministers who hide behind eloquence and the length of years they have served the Lord as pastor, preacher, or prophet, you name it. As a woman who discerns strongly, I can see what I call the *spiritual hiddenness*. This happens when the eloquent, prideful, or simply those who are ashamed hide their issues through a spiritual cover of some sort. Adam and Eve practiced this in the garden; the concept is not new. Others may be highly impressed with some of these ministers, but I pray they are healed of what I see because I have been there too! Others have discerned who I am, and I have seen right through others.

Girl, as a woman pursing the ministry path, I beseech you to get the healing, freedom, and deliverance that the Lord has already made available for you and me. We can only gain something, even if we have to put the ministry doors on hold. I can assure you that you will not regret it because it will change how you feel emotionally, mentally, spiritually, and even physically. And the outflow of the Holy Spirit will be like no other.

Are you ready to answer to the call to heal and get deliverance? Invite the Lord to minister to you and leave no area untouched. If this topic really stirs your spirit, I recommend my book, *Unapologetically Free: Deliverance and Freedom through the Spirit-filled Life*, as it covers this topic in great detail. Remember, however, that nothing can take the place of the Lord when it comes to deliverance and freedom—not my book, someone's teaching, or anything else. But they can direct you in the right path. Let's pray!

Declaration: The Father leaves no area of my spiritual and emotional life untouched. He swings doors of deliverance wide open for me over my ministry and my family. I invite the Lord to begin the work that only He can do through the power of the Holy Spirit here on earth. Jesus paid for it, the Father ordained it, and the Holy Spirit manifests it. I confess that I and everything that I have belong to Jesus Christ—my mind, my spirit, and my body. I will serve the Lord and Him alone! I declare that I break up with all work of unrighteousness. My body, spirit, and soul will be used to bring the Lord glory. I repent of ever participating in darkness of any sort, whether in false religions, doctrines, or the occult. I repent of being sexually immoral and defiling my temple. I confess to giving the enemy space in my head and heart. I dedicate my body, mind, and spirit to the Lord Jesus Christ. Every word of darkness that has ever been spoken over me is broken now by the authority and power of Jesus Christ. I will accomplish what the Lord has sent me to accomplish. I will be a vessel of love and power through the Holy Spirit. I invite the Holy Spirit to use me. In His Powerful and unmatchable name, I declare!

CHAPTER 12

GIRL, FIND THE SECRET PLACE

Regardless of where you have been with respect to a call and purpose within and outside the church walls, the Lord has not forgotten you. What may seem like delays have not been true postponements, as He has already included a plan for those things that would get in your way. Whether you caused the delays, someone you love resisted your ministry, or you suffered with a health issue, the Lord has you covered. The only thing left now is for you to pursue Him with passion in the *secret place*. The secret place is that holy and sacred location and time that you frequent as the Holy Spirit and your spirit draw you in. For most believers, this moment, place, and time are introduced by the Holy Spirit. In this moment, things like worshiping, praying, being loved by God, and loving Him will take place, and those who want to go deeper will never feel like they get enough-that is a great thing! This place is entirely God ordained, and the anointing, healing, deliverance, revelation, and character building that take place leave no room for any pastor, minister, or teacher to take credit for what happens there. The spiritual intensity of God's presence in the secret place is advanced, non-carnal, and at times unexplainable. It introduces you and me to a very forgiving, welcoming, restoring, correcting God and His love. In this place, He, the Lord, releases empowerment and activation for the ministry that you so deeply desire.

The first fifteen years of my Christian life were spent being trained in the secret place. During this season, my kids were small, and I used to drop them off at a mom's-day-out program. It enabled us moms to have several hours to ourselves a few times a week to get some things done. For me, this meant not wasting time on anything else; I just wanted to spend time with the Lord. Once I arrived back home after leaving the kiddos, I would move my living room table to where only the rug was left. On the table, I would place my Bible, a notepad, tissue, and a pen. That, my friend, was my invitation. I wanted the Lord to make Himself at home, and I was expecting to have a visitation from Him. His touch was one that only the Spirit of the Living God—the Holy Spirit—can provide. I already had a music list on my phone with songs that really spoke to my spirit and helped me tune into the presence of the Lord. I would worship until I felt filled up, or I would worship, then pray some outload in the Spirit (tongues), or I would proclaim various scriptures from the Word of God depending on the season and situations I was facing. The most amazing part of all of this was the strong pull I felt many times in a week.

My sessions with the Lord went on even after my kids were much older and I still go there today. The Song of Solomon 2:10 was playing out in my life: "My beloved responded and said to me, 'Arise, my darling, my beautiful one, And come along.'"

The Lord longs for us to come along with Him and meet Him in that place where His presence can be made manifest and can be revealed and felt. This place is not only for a special few, but only a small number seek after it. The invitation is wide open, but how many are willing to turn off the noise to make room for Him? Of course, the Lord is with you at all times, but what you experience when you make special arrangements and plans with Him can change your destiny.

Almost every one of those appointments invited a powerful,

tangible, supernatural demonstration of God's presence and power. I would often become slain in the Spirit, even if no one laid hands on me. It still happens today. I grew in my prayer language, was set free, received healing, was given answers to prayers, and so much more. Those encounters were never routine. Some things were consistent, such as the fasting, prayer and worship, but what the Lord did in each of those secret place visitations was never predictable. There were times when the Lord just received my worship, but He always made it known that He was there. If I was having a hard time sensing His presence, I would push even harder and tell Him, "I am not leaving here until You touch me." He knew exactly what that meant, and He met me there, no exceptions!

The secret place is such an intimate, private moment that many do not like talking about their experiences with anyone. While there have been some very private and for-me-only moments, how else can I make you desire the secret place if I don't at least give you a glimpse of what awaits you? These experiences, coupled with the Word of God, will equip you for ministry in a greater way than most any Bible college can unless they encourage and make room for these types of encounters. The secrete place experiences are not enough to prepare you to bring the kingdom of God here on earth, however. They *must* be coupled with the constant reading and receiving of the Word of God. Without both, we are simply carnal Christians. We may dangerously conclude that we can have an experience and not *sink into* our full identity in Christ, or we may minimize His presence and power and suppose that all we need is the Bible for our time on this earth.

One thing to know is that the secret place has seasons. There may be days in which you need lots of comfort and pats on the back and the Lord's tenderness. Others may be filled with training for warfare and proclamation. The pull for you to enter into the secret place may be stronger at some times than others. If you belong to the Lord, it will always be necessary for you to go to this intimate place. Some experiences may evolve and then lead us back to the basics.

This is a lifestyle. There is absolutely no excuse for not entering into this place, but the flesh will often resist. Sometimes, as soon as you decide you are going away with your Love for a bit, the dishes will be calling, that thing you couldn't remember you had to do this morning will suddenly be crystal clear, and the kids will be rushing in to talk to you. Be cautious with that. If it is not the external pulling; it may just be your flesh flipping out because it does not like anything that will submit to God. "For the flesh sets its desire against the Spirit, and the Spirit against the flesh; for these are in opposition to one another, so that you may not do the things that you please" (Galatians 5:17).

Notice the end of the scripture. It says that they are in opposition so that you may not do the things *you* please. That indicates that you (your spirit) actually pleases to be with the Lord. You actually desire, need, and want to spend time with Him, but your flesh wants to be in charge and would like to pull you away to the things that have no eternal value. Girl, find the secret place and make it your lifestyle.

Growth in the Lord happens beyond the secret place as well. Every time you are going to watch television or media of any kind, ask yourself if that program will increase your closeness and growth in the Lord. I still watch programs that are not related to church and growth, but I spend little time doing that. I question myself several times a week as the occasions arise if what is on at that moment is more advantageous than the book sitting on my table, or more empowering than that video I wanted to watch about a particular spiritual growth topic. In all things, women and men of God will daily have to choose what they want more than anything.

No one can make us give the important stuff up. Others may have demanding family members or a job that seems to pull on their spare time, but it's OK to set boundaries that will satisfy everyone's needs. If we are not able to do this without resistance, we usually need to set expectations down *firmly* and with consistency.

One thing I have witnessed many times over is that a large number of believers lack the depth of the secret place. They have learned the right *talk,* they have been in church long enough to prove their Christianity, and they know exactly what to say and when and how to say it. Their words are religiously sound, but when the storms hit, the first thing they do is question "Why?" Every hard season turns into a shaking of their faith and wondering if God is true or not.

Another concern is that, instead of getting into the Bible often and the secret place as a lifestyle, they take in the Word only on Sundays or midweek. They often throw a short devotion, a book, or a video into the mix, but not always. And if they are watching teachings online, they feel that can take the place of the Word of God.

Ladies, those who long to be used for greatness carry great discipline that they *choose* daily, and they take in what will empower them to the greatest level. This may seem a lot for some of you. If it is for you, in a simple prayer, ask the Lord to increase your hunger for His Word in all forms whether listening to it, reading it, or watching His Word on video. You may ask the same of the secret place. The Lord will not hold it against you. If we are completely honest, many will admit they are satisfied with where they are, and that is a choice we all get to make. Remember that man who asked Jesus what he needed to do to inherit eternal life? Mathew 19:16–22 will exemplify what I mean:

> And someone came to Him and said, "Teacher, what good thing shall I do that I may obtain eternal life?" And He said to him, "Why are you asking Me about what is good? There is *only* One who is good; but if you wish to enter into life, keep the commandments." *Then* he said to Him, "Which ones?" And Jesus said, "You shall not commit murder; You shall not commit adultery; You shall not steal; You shall not bear false witness; Honor your father and mother; and You shall love your

neighbor as yourself." The young man *said to Him, "All these things I have kept; what am I still lacking?" Jesus said to him, "If you wish to be complete, go *and* sell your possessions and give to *the* poor, and you will have treasure in heaven; and come, follow Me." But when the young man heard this statement, he went away grieving; for he was one who owned much property.

The young man was looking for a simple way to enter into eternal life; he wanted to check off only the minimum requirements. Yet he could not ignore that pull on the inside of him that there was more. Look at verse 21: "Jesus said to him, 'If you wish to be complete, go and sell your possessions and give to the poor, and you will have treasure in heaven; and come, follow Me.'" I believe he got excited at first. Maybe he thought, *I have kept all those commandments—I'm in!* But somehow he knew something was lacking so he had to keep asking questions. There is a difference between entering the kingdom of heaven and being made whole while here on earth. This young man wanted just enough, and the Lord wanted him to experience the *fullness* of knowing Him. In the same way, those who are convinced in the Lord that they are called to the ministry will answer to this powerful and life-changing invitation to find the secret place and make it a lifestyle. Choose Him daily. Your Love longs for time with you!

Declaration: It is the Lord's will that I find Him in the secret place. And, in the secret place, I will find Him as I seek Him without restraint. I command my flesh to come under the authority of the Spirit and do as I please, which is to seek and serve the Lord. I believe that Lord longs to reveal Himself to me. I adjure Him to do so. My soul, I command you to thirst and hunger after our God like my spirit does. It shall be so!

SECTION 3

ACTIVATING THE KINGDOM PURPOSE IN HER

CHAPTER 13

GIRL, OPEN YOUR MOUTH AND PROPHESY

Girl, it's time to open your mouth and prophesy over yourself. Your call demands some warfare, and we do that by speaking forth what the Lord says; that is, we prophesy. Don't think you will simply state your intentions and assume they will come with no resistance. Remember my words early on about the enemy's plan since the time of Adam and Eve? The one thing that has changed since then is that God's girls and boys are redeemed, but the satanic strategy is still the same.

If you visit the book of Mathew and read chapters three and four, you will witness our Heavenly Father speak identity over Jesus. At that point, the devil began his work in full-time mode. The battle is not only for your soul; it is for your purpose and identity here on earth. You must settle in your heart that, if Jesus was willing to give His life for you (Galatians 1:4), and if you have been given every spiritual blessing and have been sealed with His Spirit for the day of redemption (Ephesians 1:3), if the mind of Christ envelopes you to think, act, and live like Him (1 Corinthians 2:16), and if you were created for good works (Ephesians 2:10), then there is something worth fighting for in your enemy's mind.

You could be lost with no identity except the darkness that overtakes the world, with no destiny worth pursuing. You could be consumed by godless, worthless thoughts with no fruit. And you could be serving the pit of hell. Instead, you are destined to know Him and are assigned to cause others to do the same. Understand, you are a living threat! The Father, Son, Holy Spirit, angels, and demons alike know that you are *set apart*. The moment the enemy had a glimpse of your blessed destiny, the assignments against you were written in the heavenlies where demonic activity takes place. All this work has been nailed to the cross of Christ and under His feet. So, if it is nailed and done, why the resistance, the prayer, and the prophesying? Look around. While Satan is defeated, he has not been put away for good just yet, and until he is, we assert victory over all that pertains to us. To dismiss evil by saying it is nailed and forgotten is to decide to turn a blind eye. Darkness is evident everywhere, even in people's hearts, and to ignore it is not a warrior's design. Girl, you have been silent long enough. Open your mouth and prophesy!

My friend, the declaration I have included, which you are about to proclaim over yourself, is a powerful one. Most of us do not understand the power of words even though we have learned about them over and again at church or in our Christian circles. Once you get the opportunity to help someone become free from demonic oppression, you will experience a higher level of insight on just how much the devil works with words. In saying this, it is my heart's longing that you recognize that your words, or the words of others can open and shut doors, crack open the heavens, or invite the heavy glory atmosphere, and much more.

Declaration: I am a chosen vessel, filled with the Holy Spirit of God, redeemed by the blood of the Lamb, and graced by the Father's love. Reclaimed and cleansed is my current standing and position. I sit in heavenly places in the Lord Jesus Christ of Nazareth. I speak to the day I was conceived by my father's seed in my mother's womb. I release God's divine welcoming word over my life. Man's rejection cannot stand because I have a divine invitation to reside on earth for such a time as this to know the Father and bring Him great glory. Father, I assert Your grace over my life, that where words of abandonment and rejection have been spoken over me, the truth of the Lord will overtake me. I was fearfully and wonderfully made, and I command my soul to know and accept this truth now, in Jesus's name! I release the ancient plan of God over my spirit, soul, and body to decree and declare His Word boldly and fearlessly with love as His signature, followed by miracles, signs, and wonders. I am a vessel that releases the unfailing, unmatchable love of God. The glory of God is made known where I go because I welcome Him to enter each moment. I preach with the fire of the Holy Spirit that reaches deep, cleanses, heals, restores, and propels the plans of God. I prophesy, and cast out demons, and the signs follow me. I command my timing on earth to meet the timing of those who were assigned to me and I to them. The days of stagnation and barriers are over. Lord, let your love and humility be the foundation of my desires and passions and the seat of my appetites. May the expression of this declaration manifest itself today!

CHAPTER 14

GIRL, DON'T TRY MINISTRY WITHOUT THE HOLY SPIRIT

I consider this to be one of my favorite and most important chapters. Any ministry without the signature of the Holy Spirit is not a certified Jesus agency. All ministers must be best friends with the Spirit of the Lord for their lives and for the lives they will touch. The Lord desires that we awaken to the presence and the *dunamis* (a Greek word that means "power") that He carries. Without the Holy Spirit, we are simply *talking*.

What do we need so that we may grow more in the knowledge of His Spirit? We need to embrace the fact that we were meant to love and know Him as we love the Father and the Son. I love Jesus, I love the Father, and I love the Holy Spirit, but I used to feel guilty if I spent too much time acknowledging the Father over the Holy Spirit, or Jesus over the Father. The truth is that they are not in competition, and they love that you love the Holy Trinity. It is their pleasure to exalt and elevate each other. It is not like being here on earth where we are so broken that the attention of one can bring out a competitive and jealous spirit. The most unified, equal, loving, and power-filled relationship we can witness and should ponder on is that of the Father, Son, and Holy Spirit. All you have to do is read John 17 to witness it, and there are truly no words to describe it the way it deserves to be communicated. While they are equal and love one another, Jesus chose to leave us His Spirit here on earth, and He went as far as asking the Father to give us this gift. Jesus said, "I will ask the Father, and He will give you another Helper, that He may be with you forever" (John 14:16).

He requested this of the Father on behalf of you and me. I give equal praise and love to the Father, Son, and Holy Spirit, but I am very aware that, without the Holy Spirit, ministries remain on a first-level basis, the carnal level.

Women of God, one of the most important things you can do is develop your relationship with the Holy Spirit, that you may begin to discern His presence, His work, His healing, His salvation, and His deliverance. He will be the *One* who reveals Jesus to a crowd of broken, deceived individuals. His job is to break the chains and cast out demons. He can grow an arm, raise the dead, heal the sick, and so much more. Acts 1:8 confirms that we serve an all-powerful, divine, and supernatural Father and Son: "But you will receive power when the Holy Spirit has come upon *you*, and *you* will be my witnesses in Jerusalem and in all Judea and Samaria, and to the end of the earth."

This scripture points to evangelism and to the manifestation of His power and presence. To be a witness means that you will testify to what someone did or did not do. The only testimony we have of the Father, Son, and Holy Spirit is that which is in the Bible, and there is no lack of power that we can testify to! We can, however, bear witness that one of God's greatest generals, the Apostle Paul, set the tone for ministry when he made it clear that, without the *demonstration* of the Spirit's power, there is nothing but persuasive words of the wisdom of humankind as stated in 1 Corinthians 2:4–5: "And my message and my preaching were not in persuasive words of wisdom, but in demonstration of the Spirit and of power, so that your faith would not rest on the wisdom of men, but on the power of God."

Depending on fancy words and eloquent speeches can open us

up to pride because we will not depend on the Lord, but primarily on our abilities and giftings. The Holy Spirit is the One who will open the heavens and release the manifested presence of the Lord, so learn to get out of His way that He may do just that.

For years, we have seen the evidence of many men in ministry and even some women resting on their own wisdom. They may have worked hard at their studies, read countless works and books, and daily chased after *knowledge*. There is not much wrong with that except it is unacceptable to couple our acquisition of knowledge with a denial that the Holy Spirit still reveals Jesus on earth with *power* and then lead others to believe the same. While the Lord has ministered, even through those who deny His power, it was not for them that He did it, but for those who needed a hope and an encouraging word. The full gospel, however, carries manifested power. Never was ministry intended to be accomplished through our eloquent words or preaching alone. A large number of individuals who are passionately against women ministers also resist the present operation of the Holy Spirit. They deny that His work is still being accomplished here on earth with evidence of power—gifts and other supernatural evidence—and they deny women their right to the kingdom of God. Is that not interesting, or simply a coincidence? I highly doubt it is a coincidence.

We must be very careful not to be so sure in our own understanding and assume the Lord is *not* still moving here on earth upon humankind. Besides the evidence we have in the Bible that the Holy Spirit is still active *today* for the sake of the saved and the unsaved, we have also experienced power-filled events that support the biblical testimonies. This undeniable power is made available only by the Holy Spirit as it belongs to Him!

Let's be women who seek after a relationship *first* followed by encounters with Him. As we see and walk through more doors for the girls, be prepared to be a vessel for the fullness of the Holy Spirit. There are many who are out there serving the Lord, but they want to serve Him *without* the presence and power of the Holy

Spirit. A woman ministering without communion with the Holy Spirit and His participation is simply a woman *working*. A preacher, pastor, prophet, evangelist, apostle, teacher, or minister in complete involvement with the Spirit of the Living God is a woman who walks by the revelation power of the Lord. Seek Him first, become acquainted with who He is to you, then He will instruct you in the rest. He loves to train; that is why He is called the *Teacher* in 1 John 2:27. Ask Him to teach you to be His friend, to be a lover of Jesus and a child of the Father. His great pleasure will be to enlighten you and demonstrate to you just how real the Father, Son, and Holy Spirit are here on earth.

I have wept, begged, and pleaded that He not ever allow me to do ministry without His presence. It would be a shame to get out there in my own ability. I have done it before when I first started in ministry, but I was very aware of what I was missing. In the secret place and in pursuing the manifest presence of the Lord is where I learned just how available the Lord was making Himself for me and for His tribe. If I can make known to you just how beautiful and necessary knowing the Holy Spirit is for you and the ministry you will carry, then you will be one more successful woman of God carrying out her kingdom purpose.

We can't afford to be in partnership with a counterfeit. Anything that attempts to represent the Lord and His kingdom here on earth without the current ministry of the Holy Spirit is just a false representation of whom we say God is. And, girl, remember that darkness never went away, it does still have its work here on earth. I have been bound to deception and have played with darkness and its power, as have many others. It is real, and if the power of evil is real, how much more the dunamis of the Creator of heaven and earth? Be filled with the Spirit, girl, emptied of yourself, and watch how the Lord pours Himself out through you!

As I mentioned before, get to know Him yourself first. Talk to Him, acknowledge His presence when you wake up, talk to Him about anything you desire. Invite the Holy Spirit to reveal what you are not aware of in your own life. As you begin to know Him for yourself, be sure you invite Him to enter the moment or environment by His own desire, which you certainly will want. Pray in tongues as often as possible, make it a lifestyle. That is, after all, His language. Welcome Him to increase your awareness of the Love of the Father, the grace of Jesus, and His fellowship. Tell Him you want to go to deeper places in Him that you have never experienced before. He will surely lead the way. If you request that He remove the boundaries that religion and tradition have enforced around your beliefs, He will. Once you begin to be so filled with Him, He will *naturally* overflow out of you. You will not be able to contain His presence or His power. This is a supernatural event! Girl, don't try ministry without the Holy Spirit!

Declaration: The Holy Spirit is the source of my ministry. He reveals Jesus and the Father to those who come into contact with me. He overflows in me, and His work is ever present and pours out as a holy and consuming fire. I will not deny the present movement and work of the Holy Spirit. He alone teaches me what is God and what is man. I cannot contain His presence and will not get in His way. I decree that the Holy One will walk into the moment no matter where I am or who I am ministering to. He will make Himself known—Father, Son, and Holy Spirit!

CHAPTER 15

GIRL, DON'T KEEP SILENT! PREACH!

G irl, I trust you have noticed that, as American women, we are free. We vote, are VPs, start and run successful businesses, sign up as soldiers, keep homes, and then some. The positions we fill are unlimited even if the numbers are still few but growing in certain industries. We cannot say the same for the American woman in the church, although it is not limited to us as Americans. Others of our sisters in Christ across the globe are still under oppression whether they are choosing a career, picking out their own wardrobe, going out in public without a male figure, and other endeavors. They certainly are not living out the freedom Jesus Christ has paid for them in all manner of respects. That should move us all to pray and find a way to empower them. An uncountable number of women who are made in the image of God do not even get to choose their own faith *practices*. Of course, they can choose Jesus in their hearts, but they do not have the permission to practice as they please and would take pleasure in doing.

Interestingly, American women preachers and teachers are, in some ways, in the same position as women in dictatorial countries because oppression is also played out within the walls of Christian churches. This may sound extreme, but if we ponder on it, we will see the similarities between the two. In both situations, women are limited because they are *females* and are forced to limited spiritual boundaries.

This, my girls, when seen beyond the traditions and religious expectations, is really a spiritual war against women. Look past this dilemma and you will find that multitudes of the 1 Corinthians 14 "no women preachers" subscribers actually deny the gifts listed in 1 Corinthians 12. They don't bother to pursue greater understanding for either one. They pick and choose and use their chosen ideas against the very women whom God elected. To put it in a visual perspective, allow me to ask you this: What would happen if women preached to men or if they were present while men unapologetically presented the Word of the Lord? Would our brothers' ears wither if you and I speak? Would their hearts turn away from the Lord?

The level of callousness of the heart that has to be present in order to deny a woman her God-given right to preach is immense, and men and women can both be accomplices. Girl, even with all of the impediments present, you have no excuse to be silent. In our great nation, nothing can force you to silence your preaching, prophesying, teaching, pastoring, evangelizing, leading apostolically, and anything else you are mantled for. While many pastors and ministers are holding the keys to these positions that are supposed to be filled within the church walls by the men and women of God, they will have to give an account as will you and I for the preaching we *didn't* do.

I have gone in search of the doors and opportunities to preach, and I have found many in ways you and I would not expect or imagine. Access will come with obedience. A door won't open? Knock on the next one, but you'd better preach! Women from the turn of the twentieth century to our present time have found ways to get to walk out the anointing in their lives. They all, in their own books and messages, have shared that their journey was challenging when they first got started and even after years of ministering. We are forever grateful for the courageous women who came before us. Let us rise and not be willing to succumb to the pressure of remaining silent "in the name of God." These brave women gave it all they had, and some of them even sacrificed their children's welfare so that you and I would not have to do the same. They endured the cold, the heat, the hunger, the death of a husband, the sneers, the confrontations, and the general demonic wrestling hidden behind well-meaning people of God and the purposefully evil. Put yourself in their shoes for a moment. Don't you think they may have been fearful? Intimidated but still kept preaching? Scared for their children but they asked themselves, "If not me, then who?" We are in a 2 Chronicles 16:9 moment: "For the eyes of the Lord move to and fro throughout the earth that He may strongly support those whose heart is completely His."

The Lord will strongly support you and me when our hearts are given full access to Him. Some of us have been graced for this assignment as some of our female preacher predecessors were. This moment in time groans for those who may have some fear but are still brave. It calls for that woman who will say, "Send me, Lord." We owe it to these past and present day Deborahs, Phoebes, Priscillas, Annas, and beyond to *unapologetically* answer the internally compelling invitation of the Holy Spirit to release the divine within us. Pray and ask for the courage! It's your season, girl!

Declaration: I will stand for what the Father's heart longs to see come to pass here on earth concerning His girls. His eyes move to and fro upon my life, so I invite Him to find me faithful and willing. I invite Him to strongly support me. I declare that the Lord will find me, send me, use and equip me. The words that come out of my mouth will be filled with the Holy Spirit, charged with His holy fire to awaken, ignite, and release the women who are silently waiting to be called upon—those girls who have not embraced that they, too, are part of the Father's unapologetic call for women on the earth. I will no longer live a safe, Christian life. May the fearless Spirit of the Lord overtake me for Him!

CHAPTER 16

GIRL, LET THE DOORS OPEN NOW

So you have prophetic words that were given to you years ago, your Bible study time is firmly set, the secret place is scheduled weekly, you have read the endless books regarding a call and a purpose, you've subscribed to all the newsletters offered, you enrolled in the online school of ministry, and now you just want to know what is the Lord waiting on, right?

Most of you have gone through the process of hearing the call, entering into a spiritual development season of days, months, and even years, and yet feel as if you have been in a long holding pattern. After all, you were promised the open doors, international travel, the ability to heal the sick, and all the rest that comes with this territory. This process can feel very frustrating; it can cause major ongoing doubt about the promises God has made to you and me. For some, it may even cause unreasonable disappointment with the Lord.

All those who believe the Lord called them to great assignments, if they are honest, will tell you that they too have struggled with what feels like a delay on the Lord's part. Then there are those who were called and not long after salvation seem to have begun working in the ministry, but the truth is the Lord had been preparing them, just in a different way than He did people like you and me.

We all go through a preparation time; it just looks different for everyone. One group of people may have been training as servants of Christ in the shadows of another. They have learned to assist the ministers of God whom the Father put in their lives. Admirably, instead of trying to be those they assist, they have worked to simply give their best and learn and glean all that they can for that season from that assignment. Through this process they have become well acquainted with the ropes having to do with respect, honor, holiness, faithfulness, and hard work. They applied themselves even on hard days, with or without applause, and have pushed beyond false accusations. This shadow training put them at the forefront of many people, platforms, and opportunities that others see as desirable. But we may not understand the work and character that it took to be trusted *there*. Both those who have learned in the full-time ministry of serving another and those who have been trained in the cave have been prepared and processed through a spiritual and character training that is unavoidable. All of these individuals have had to wait on the Lord and be faithful to Him no matter what environment they have been made ready in. I personally have been in the training of the Lord's secret place, which oftentimes feels like being in eternal hiddenness. The Lord will hide you away, and the Holy Spirit will teach you many things. Either He trains you in the quiet, away from others, or He puts you at the service of a trailblazer. In life, these can happen together or separately at different times. It is vital that you willingly ready yourself because preparation goes before open doors!

THE PLATFORM

Public ministry is really just ministering to anyone who needs to be touched by the Living God. We have been sold into the American gospel, which always carries the superstar mentality, which means me plus a public platform equals ministry. Don't wait for an overrated stage. Let the doors open now! Ask the Lord to give you the urge to serve Him daily where there is need. This will keep you in fulltime ministry with no public outlet needed. This can sound like a bummer to those who have been dreaming of the public doors. And, while I know the Lord can present and may be providing the outlets for you and me, it never disqualifies being faithful where we are.

One of the ways I have tried to stay faithful to the Lord since my early days in ministry is to put public events together myself. I hosted the opportunity whether I was in my young-mom season and equipping other stay-at-home moms or my kids-are-a-bit-older stage and serving the men and women of God who really needed to be encouraged from time to time.

As long as you operate in your anointing, you can serve the Lord in many capacities. He may tell you to stop performing particular activities after a certain season, but for the most part, we can continue to serve Him in what we have been anointed to do until He feels we are prepared for the next level. We will never be ready for the upgrade, however, until we maximize our training and our doing in the current season. Remember the disciples? What were they doing when Jesus found them? They were busy!

I, like many, found my calling by *doing*. It happened in stages. When my husband and I moved to the town we currently live in, I hated it. I am from a big city where there is a book store or library at a reasonable distance from home, a grocery store at every corner, and people everywhere. Moving to what was, at that time, a suburb was too lonesome and quiet for me, so I had to find something to do. I contacted my local library and asked them what they needed help doing. I was willing to dust the books if needed, but with no job, no friends, and no family near me, I needed to connect or depression would overtake me. They asked about my skills and abilities, and we came to an agreement that I would teach Spanish, which I had never done before! I could speak it and write it some, and that was good enough for them. I put a lesson together, showed up, and realized afterward how much I loved to teach adults.

Other things happened after and even in between this moment that reinforced my call and gifting, but I found my love for teaching during a period of depression and loneliness because I was not willing to continue feeling that way. I began to hold events and extend opportunities for others to develop and express their talents and expand their businesses and ministries. Through elevating others, I discovered more about the Lord's giftings in me. As I engaged in empowering those around me, a revelation of my preaching nature unfolded.

Obviously so much more has followed, including television ministry and writing, but all this happened because I was willing to do just one thing—step out even when I was not fully sure which way to go. I have not always been comfortable with all that has been presented to me, but I did it even though I felt afraid, and at times I still do. I have a wild determination to be used by the Lord, and where I want to be used, I will give my all. I may run into discouraging days, challenges, and lack of motivation every so often, and that is OK.

Today was one of those days. Just before I began to write this chapter, I spoke with a friend who has fathered and encouraged me in many situations. He heard my discouragement, and he admonished me, "Grind and don't let up!" By the time our conversation was over, I felt I could accomplish anything.

While I don't have a secret solution to the waiting season, I know very intimately the fight for staying faithful even if the crickets are louder than the action related to His promises. If the promise is from Him, you will have the internal strength to hang on even if every so often you feel like letting go.

We have been taught to constantly seek the next thing, never being able to fully enjoy where we are. The Lord is not lost; He has already calculated the quiet days into your schedule. He knows where to find us at the right time. The Lord is very familiar with impatient people who have a promise. Just look at the story of Abraham and Sarah in the Bible.

Also, keep a lookout for seasons of betrayal, heartache, loss, and other unpleasant situations, as promotion can often be packaged in those periods of life. Just look back at the life of Joseph.

I am guilty of assuming that open doors of growth and elevation look like pleasant gifts; yet, realistically they can present themselves in an uncomfortable manner. We have plenty of evidence for that in the Bible. Don't be discouraged. Remember to serve wholeheartedly in the now in the territory you have been given. Many need what you carry *right now*.

I have to visit my own words from time to time no doubt, so I am preaching to myself. The most important lesson I pray you take from this section, however, is that, if you do anything according to what you are anointed to do, you will experience the satisfaction and God fulfillment you think you have had to wait for! There is no way I could have written this book and other books without the waiting, the praying and the grinding, and without faithfulness. Let your life preach, girl, in your waiting, in your doing, and in your being!

TEACHING OTHERS TO OPEN THEIR DOORS

Pouring into others what they may need for their own growth is another activity we should attempt to do in the waiting and fulfilling of the current season. There are many Christ followers who are hungry to possess what you know and to understand what you have had the privilege of experiencing. What would you say if I asked you what you have done for others lately to equip and help grow their territory? Ministry is equipping, and it can start there!

Not long ago, I had the great privilege of being on a television program that airs in a country where women are not allowed to live like free human beings with rights to pursue a career, ministry, or any other endeavor; all they are allowed to do is bear children and care for their men. These women are restricted to meeting in one another's homes and not much else. The television show host, a well-known man, asked me to share with the women what they could do to pursue their God-given call and purpose even when they are limited by such restrictions in the name of their god and government. In that moment, I encouraged the women to find what they are naturally passionate about. I asked them to think about what gives them joy, even in that restricted place. Was it cooking meals and coming up with creative recipes? Then I encouraged them to host cooking classes in their homes. Was it writing poems? They should invite women to learn how to develop in the area of creative writing. The goal was to work within the guidelines of the governmental and religious confinements that currently exist and still operate in their anointing, gifting, and call. There is still room in a restrictive environment, and we will find it if we seek it.

Declaration: Let the doors open wide according to the will and harvest that has been assigned to me. No door shall remain hidden or closed. I command the divine opportunities and the timing of the Lord to line up. I come into agreement with all that the Lord has appointed and anointed me for. The lost will meet the Savior and embrace their destiny through my willing availability and obedience to the Lord. Let the Lord release His angels to coordinate heaven's assignments here on earth!

CHAPTER 17

GIRL, RECEIVE THE BLESSING

irl, you have been equipped with a theological foundation. The keys that take you deeper are now in your hand, and you know what it takes to activate the kingdom purpose in you. At this point, I pray there has been a major revelation in your soul about the way the Lord feels about you as His daughter and as His servant minister. There is no one created just like you, even though we are all created in God's image.

Imagine a mother who conceived and carried her baby for months. Imagine the point at which she experienced life within her. She felt the baby's presence and knew without a doubt that her child would one day become someone great. Sadly, the baby does not make it. In time, she heals from the pain of the loss, has another baby, and continues on with life. While she may have given birth to another blessing, that baby will never take the place of the one she lost. The newest addition will bring her own presence, blessing, and life to this family, but never will take the other baby's place because the Lord created it that way.

That is how He feels about you and your purpose on earth. Don't be so quick to give it up to the pressures of the divided Christian faith. I have to pull at your heartstrings because many of us, including men and women, have heard about how worthless we are because we were bought with a price. We are taught unfruitful religious talk from early on in our Christian lives. I have to ask you—would you pay a huge price for something without value? I realize that I didn't earn Jesus's sacrifice, but I know that the Father loved me and you enough to give us all He had—Jesus.

So how can we constantly reduce ourselves to worms? If I reduce who I am to practically nothing, I will never believe that the Lord desires to be with me. One thing I know now after much time in the secret place is that He longs to be with me. He awaits my undivided attention to minister to Him, meaning to just love on Him. At His feet, I can pour my affection on Him for the way He brought me into His family when I was a lost woman. He never rejected me, even when I used Him to bail me out of my messes time after time. How can I not pour out abundant praise and worship?

He loves to love me, and in those moments when you learn to create the atmosphere in which you and God can have a personal encounter, you will heal from the pain and disappointment you carry because you are a girl and have not been given the freedom to let the Lord out of your vessel. Those who have been through deep wounds will fully understand the healing our soul cries out for. The refusal of others to welcome God's girls can actually cause a self-rejection spirit or other spiritual bondage such as bitterness and unforgiveness, as well as hate toward men, toward the church, or toward Christians in general.

My friends, that ought not to be. The Lord wants to heal you, and though His healing is the beginning of your moving forward, at times you may not be aware that is what is missing in your life. In my invitation for you to experience some healing, I have a story I want to share. While I have been restored in my soul from so much brokenness that I invited in, and from that which I did not personally welcome, the Lord continues to point out areas that still demand healing within. I understand that, without a constant submission to comfort, correction, and healing, we cannot be the most loving and effective ministers for the Lord. Being aware of this truth, I knew I had an old wound that had recently opened wide. I put my guard down, not fully having the evidence that this particular situation merited my trust. Rejection, abandonment, and the spirit of partiality came full force to try and put me in bondage once again to something I had learned to cope with. The issue is, the Lord didn't just want me to learn to endure the pain and sweep it away to hide it. This time, the wound was meant to be healed. I was honest with my Father in heaven. I told Him about the pain, the hurt, and the disappointment.

After that day, I got myself together and decided to keep moving forward. Within several days, while writing a newsletter for my email subscribers, I felt I needed to write a prayer for the readers. The Holy Spirit said to me in such a loud voice in my spirit, "Write the prayer as if I am writing it." I said, "Lord, but the religious people will get all worked up and accuse me of trying be You." He said, "Write it." I said, "Yes, Lord. I know I need to get over what anyone has to say anyway." I began writing a prayer in first person as if it was spoken by the Lord. The moment I started to write the blessing, I knew it was for me first. I wrote and wept, and wrote, and wept. I had to stop several times because the Holy Spirit would allow me to take in His healing filled with love and compassion for the pain that had accompanied me for years and years. As I was writing the very last line of the prayer, I was about to end it with "So be healed, my child." But the Lord said, "No, write, 'so be healed, my daughter.'" He was speaking to me personally. He wanted this to be my personal blessing and healing first before I released it to the public.

Surely at this point you have figured out that I am a bit persistent, so I was about to say, "Lord, but this is for the public." And He said, "Write 'my daughter.'" Do I need to tell you about the river I cried at this moment? I could hear the Lord speak so clearly to me. He was pursuing my healing more than my soul was, but it was a bit uncomfortable so I was not pushing as hard as I would with other things. This emotional injury had nothing to do with the subject of my book, but I know His healing intimately enough to understand that the healing principles can overlap and overflow into other areas of our lives.

I knew that the prayer that He spoke over me was to be included in this chapter. Just imagine it—the Living God manifested His voice loud enough for me to hear Him blessing me so that I could heal. He wants to do the same for you, He told me so. While some of your hurts may have to do with rejection as a woman, it may also have to do with afflictions you may or may not have identified. Are you readying your heart to enter the healing room as I share my own story?

I took one other step before making this prayer public. I shared it with several women who are on my prayer team, and they too experienced a deep level of healing and comfort they were not expecting. Some of them read it several times over. I did so also until I knew by the Lord's confirmation that He had taken care of all the pieces connected to my pain. It's not a long prayer because length is not the point—it's His power. Take this journey with the Lord yourself. Don't hurry yourself, though. Rushing will not be productive. Sit at His feet and watch the Holy Spirit's power and presence pour out all over your heart. If you read it and don't experience anything, try it again another time. Here we go!

THE BLESSING PRAYER

My child, I love you. I love to love you. I gave my most precious Son for you, to show you just how much I wanted My love, kindness, and forgiveness to overflow in your life, to show you that, even in the darkest of days, when you ran to the pit instead of to Me, I waited on you. My intentions are good, and I replace them, at this moment, over and above the intentions and plans of the enemy. Even when I have seemed quiet, not present, as if you were alone, I was with you. I was watching you, calling and drawing you to My heart. I deeply desired that you would have a small, tiny, glimpse of my love and purifying presence. I spoke to the angels I created. I looked at them, and they looked at me, and they knew how much I wanted you to know the love I have for you. They were dismissed from my presence to yours that they would coordinate an opportunity for you to enter into a moment in which you could encounter Me. This happened over and again until, one day, I saw you raise your head and begin to "feel me." You allowed the voice of your anger and fear to drown for a moment so that I could comfort you. I held you as you fell in your pain. As your wounds surfaced, you fell into My arms. You didn't realize it at first until you started to feel the comfort. You didn't realize it, but when you stopped crying, at that moment, it was My comfort that washed over you. I held you. My heart hurt for you, but I knew you would be fine because you would come back to Me. I see your deep wounds—wounds of not feeling sufficiently loved by those you want love from the most. I see that you want to withdraw from life and people because that would feel safe, but it is not. Come to the place of healing. Cry in My arms and receive wisdom and understanding for your situations. I am holding you, even when it does not seem so. Come to Me and allow Me to comfort you. I love you. Even in the crying, there is healing. So be *healed*, my daughter.

Read through this prayer as many times as you need to until you hear the Lord tell you He is finished. You will know when to call it done! Now inhale the breath of relief and freedom.

At the end of it all, the most important ministry is to know and love the Lord. Nothing else. It truly does not matter if you are a man or a woman in ministry when the true purpose for living has not been discovered. The blessing is to commune with Him and seek Him above all else, after which all other things will be endowed to you. You were made to worship, and out of the worship and deep place of encounter, it will be easy to be the blessing upon someone else. Depth will come forth from you, and people will hunger after that which is in you, the Lord Jesus Christ. There are plenty of options out there, but none compare to Him. Girl, just don't forget to preach, teach, prophecy, evangelize, lead apostolically or otherwise with all that is within you! Your kingdom purpose awaits you!

CHAPTER 18

PRAYERS THAT HEAL US GIRLS

A s I prayed about what to include at the end of this book, I felt it would be good to reach out to a few trusted men in my life who carry strong convictions for the *unrestricted* ministry of women and ask them each to share a prayer for the women. The prayers that I have included have been carefully composed by these great brothers in the Lord! The words submitted are verbatim as they sent them to me since I asked them to prayerfully compose every blessing.

I believe that the Father will heal the hearts of many daughters who could use a kind, affirming, loving word of encouragement. Some prayers are from a first-person perspective, while others may be a prayer over you, or a combination of both. While we are not to seek the validation of others, affirmation is a powerful thing, even if it comes from those who are not responsible for our pain.

Read through each prayer and allow the Holy Spirit to point to any buried offenses or wounds that have been swept to a hiding place, sleeping dreams and calls, and any other matters that demand an awakening. May you find strength to abandon the hunger of the approval of man and energetically activate your gifting, call, and anointing for God's kingdom purpose today as you receive these prayers that heal!

WOMEN, COHEIRS IN CHRIST BY LEON LUSK

Father, Thank You that men *and* women were created to have dominion over the earth (Genesis 1:26–28). Thank You that, after the resurrection, wives will no longer be ruled over by insecure men (Mathew 22:28). Thank You that Your will is being done *now* just as it is in heaven (Mathew 6:10)! So be it! Amen.

A PRAYER FOR WOMEN-LED MINISTRIES BY MIKE DUBÉ SR.

Heavenly Father, I pray You remove from our hearts anything not of You and that we are not blinded by insecurities, bigotries, or false teachings, but are given the power of discernment that is anchored in Your Word. Lord, I pray that we support Your women-led ministries with open hearts and minds, and that our eyes are open to the truth, and that You remove any roadblocks or confusion. I pray that we come together in a spirit of unity and inclusion with support and encouragement for them.

Lord, I pray that their voices are heard mightily throughout the world; that Your blessing flows freely over them; that Your people would be strengthened and healed by You, through them; and that others would come to know Your voice. I pray that Your Word will flow from their mouths and fill open ears with the truth that glorifies You.

Father, I pray that they will be examples and leaders to others around the world of Your goodness and mercy, that they will cause others to rise up against the enemy, that strongholds will be removed, and that Your glory will shine through them.

I pray that You bless the work that they set their hands to and that it bears much fruit for Your kingdom. In Jesus's name. Amen!

A PRAYER FOR ALL THE WOMEN IN MINISTRY
BY REVEREND GLEN H. GABBARD

Dear Father God, we come to You today in the name of Your only begotten Son, the Lord Jesus Christ, on behalf of all the called-out, chosen, and anointed women you have called into Your ministry. First of all, bless and encourage them today. Undergird them with strength for the journey for which You have called them. Open doors of ministry that no man or principality can shut. Hear our prayer today, O Lord.

Dear Father, first of all, we are thankful that we are living under the new covenant as Christ fulfilled the old with His death on the cross. It is a better covenant that says that our God is no respecter of persons (Acts 10:34), and reminds us that there is no Jew or Greek, male or female (Galatians 3:28). Thank you, Father, that we are all one in Christ Jesus. Then, Lord, You gave us several practical examples of women involved in ministry in the New Testament: (1) Devout women were the first on the scene at Christ's resurrection and were entrusted with the task of telling not only the disciples but everyone that Christ has risen! (2) On the day of Pentecost, as we read in Acts 2, several noted women were included in the Upper Room prayer meeting, including Mary, the mother of Jesus. (3) Philip the evangelist had five daughters who prophesied in Acts 21:9. The word *prophecy* is defined as "speech inspired by God," which is what preaching is supposed to be!. (4) Aquila's wife, Priscilla, instructed the preacher named Apollos "in a more excellent way." Many believe she preached to him and led him to the baptism of the Holy Spirit (Acts 18:24–26)!

Now, Lord, we pray for understanding and rightly dividing the Word of God. There are admittedly two passages in the New Testament in the Corinthian writing of Paul about a woman "keeping silent" in the church and then in 1 Timothy 2:12 concerning a woman teaching a man. But, Lord, help us to see that these passages are about culture, not commandments. Women were sorely oppressed in Bible days and up into recent history. They could not be educated, could not own property, could not vote, were considered chattel property of men, and were generally mistreated and considered second-class citizens. Culture dictated for them to remain quiet, as they had no opportunities to learn and comment on the important issues of the day. Dear Lord, we understand that there are no second-class citizens in the kingdom of God! Whatever knowledge of the world women of the past may have lacked has been more than made up by the divine power and anointing of the Holy Spirit of God! Thank You, Jesus, that You have given women a voice in these last days regardless of what culture would say! Praise God!

Thank You, Lord, for the insight You have given on this important issue. Thank You for redeeming us with Your precious blood and calling us into Your ministry, both men and women alike. You instructed in Your Word that what You make clean we should not call common (Acts 10:15). So, God, I pray that You would send forth an army of women in ministry to reach a lost and hurting world in these last days. I pray that You would loose the closed pulpits that women face, and that all leadership understands that a woman's place is anywhere that God wants her to be! May all honor, glory, power, and honor be unto the Most High God! *Hallelujah and amen!*

SCRIPTURE REFERENCES BY CHAPTER

Section 1: A Girl's Guide to Biblical Truths

Introduction:
Mark 16:15–18
Hebrews 3
1. Girl, Is It Tradition or Truth?
    2 Corinthians 2:11
2. Girl, Your Worth Existed Before the Beginning of Time
    Genesis 1:27
    Genesis 3:6
    Galatians 3:28
    1 Peter 2:9
3. Girl, Who Condemns You?
    None listed
4. Girl, It's a Husband-and-Wife Thing
    Genesis 2:18–21
    Genesis 3:20
    Ephesians 5:21
    1 Corinthians 7:4
    Ephesians 5:31-33
    Ephesians 5:22-24
    Ephesians 5
    1 Samuel 25
    Genesis 21

1 Samuel 1

5. Girl, There is Evidence for Women in Leadership Positions
   1 Timothy 2:9-15
   1 Corinthians 14:34–35
   Mark 16:15–18
   2 Timothy 2:15
   Romans 16:7
   Romans 16
   1 Chronicles 17:6
   Luke 2:36
   Exodus 15:20
   2 Kings 22:14
   Romans 16:1–2
   Mark 5:11–20
   John 4
   Acts 18:24–26
   1 Timothy 2:12
   1 Corinthians 14:34–35
   1 Timothy 2:1–14
   1 Corinthians 11:5

6. Girl, Join the Godly Social Justice Cause in the Church
   None listed

7. Girls, There's Room for You Too
   John 2
   Ephesians 4:12
   Luke 2:19

8. Girl! Stop Promoting the Demonic Agenda
   Matthew 9:29
   Joel 2:28

Section 2: Things Girls Need to Know to Go Deeper

9. Girl, Answer to Your Unlikely Call
   Genesis 37

10. Girl, You Are Anointed
   2 Corinthians 2:15
   Galatians 3:28
11. Girl, Get You Some Deliverance
   Ephesians 1:6–7
   Ephesians 4:30
12. Girl, Find the Secret Place
   Song of Solomon 2:10
   Galatians 5:17
   Matthew 19:16–22

Section 3. Activating the Kingdom Purpose in Her

13. Girl, Open Your Mouth and Prophesy
   Matthew 3
   Matthew 4
   Galatians 1:4
   Ephesians 1:3
   1 Corinthians 2:16
   Ephesians 2:10
14. Girl, Don't Try Ministry Without the Holy Spirit
   John 17
   John 14:16
   Acts 1:8
   1 Corinthians 2:4–5
   1 John 2:27
15. Girl, Don't Keep Silent! Preach!
   1 Corinthians 14
   1 Corinthians 12
   2 Chronicles 16:9
16. Girl, Let The Doors Open Now
   None listed
17. Girl, Receive the Blessing
   None listed

18. Prayers that Heal Us Girls
    Genesis 1:26–28
    Mathew 22:28
    Mathew 6:10
    Acts 10:34
    Galatians 3:28
    Acts 2
    Acts 21:9
    Acts 18:24–26
    1 Timothy 2:12
    Acts 10:15

AUTHOR BIOGRAPHY

An ordained minister and powerful preacher, Teresa Lusk is the author of *Unapologetically Free: Deliverance and Freedom Through the Spirit-Filled Life, Prayers That Change Us,* and several other excellent reads. Teresa's passion is to stir the believer, break religious traditions in the church, and awaken men and women in the fullness of the love and power of Jesus Christ.

Teresa's most recent work, *Girl, Preach: A Woman's Call to Kingdom Purpose,* is an inspiration to women, encouraging them to learn to answer the undeniable call of God to minister in any capacity, both inside and outside of the church walls. She strongly believes that the same Lord who equipped her to preach His good news is the same Lord who works to heal, prophesy, and cast out demons. He wants to do these things not only through men but through women as well.

Today, Teresa is the president of Teresa Lusk Ministries, a non-profit focused on the supernatural life in Christ. She actively empowers the church to welcome the presence and power of the Holy Spirit through the laying on of the hands, healing, casting out demons, speaking in tongues, and so much more. Although her ministry is based in North Texas, she has traveled internationally and plans to continue going global to spread the fire of God. Through conferences, leadership workshops, social media, and ministry training, Teresa continues to grow this vision and lead others to freedom in Christ.

Teresa and her husband, Leon, have 3 kids and reside in the Dallas area. To learn more about Teresa, visit her website, www.teresalusk.com, or engage with her ministry on social media, @teresaluskministries.

ALSO BY TERESA G. LUSK

- Unapologetically Free: Deliverance and Freedom through the Spirit-Filled Life
- Prayers that Change Us
- Winning Favor with People God's Way
- Good Enough to be a Homemaker and CEO

Visit www.teresalusk.com for more information